For Love of the World

A Call to Canadian Catholics

Linda Marie Arbour

For Love of the World

Copyright © 2017 by Linda Marie Arbour

No part of this publication may be reproduced, distributed, or transmitted in any form or by any means, including photocopying, recording, or other electronic or mechanical methods, without the prior written permission of the author, except in the case of brief quotations embodied in critical reviews and certain other non-commercial uses permitted by copyright law.

Tellwell Talent
www.tellwell.ca

ISBN
978-1-77302-469-1 (Paperback)
978-1-77302-470-7 (eBook)

Tales Out of School

TABLE OF CONTENTS

Preface v

Chapter One
Lay Participation Matters: from orthodoxy to orthopraxis 1

Chapter Two
The Jesus of History and the Christ of Faith 11

Chapter Three
Pro-life and Anti-life Religious Consciousness 37

Chapter Four
The Dysfunction of Monastic Spirituality 47

Chapter Five
The Coming of Age of the Laity 61

Chapter Six
Mary of Nazareth 81

Chapter Seven
A Spirituality of Engagement 103

Chapter Eight
Spiritual and Material Poverty: How are they related? 121

Chapter Nine
A Parish that Matters 127

Addendum 149

About the Author 150

PREFACE

Until the arrival of Pope Francis, this theological perspective was regarded with suspicion by Catholic publishers in Canada, whereas in the United States, these ideas are more fully integrated into parish life as well as in academic circles. Through these essays, I address these concerns to the Catholic laity, because the clergy have known about these emphases for decades now and yet the only enculturation that has occurred in Canadian life has been in some Catholic secondary schools and universities. As one of the first laywomen in Toronto trained in theology after Vatican Two, my reputation and motivations in pressing for an urgent response to this new theology were repeatedly attacked by ex-religious, gay and straight, and clergy who assume that only someone with a personal axe to grind would feel so strongly about such things. With Francis as pope, I feel vindicated. The history that led up to a collective and communitarian understanding of salvation is over a century old, but is unknown to most of the faithful except for academic theologians who tend not to act on this understanding. These essays are directed to lay Catholics who want to know what is going on at the intellectual or theological level of Church life. None of this is new for academic theologians who have lived this shift in Catholic self-understanding.

In the last half of the nineteenth century in Europe, a small group of influential bishops, priests and educated laymen began to address the impact of industrialization on the family life of the urban working poor. Coming from Germany, France, Belgium, Switzerland and Italy, they met to discuss their local initiatives at the university of Fribourg in Switzerland, and out of this new consciousness came the first social encyclical, Rerum Novarum (Of New Things) and a new European-based movement called Social Catholicism. This movement shifted attention from Christianity as a quest for personal salvation and wellbeing expressed through an emphasis on almsgiving or material charity to a quest for righteousness and justice in the biblical sense, for the good of all, through democratic and legislated means. Jesus was not a monk retreating from the challenges of the street and he doesn't appear to have been much interested in social upward mobility. He was an observant Jew who allowed the words of the sacred writings of his religious tradition to seep into his being and to shape his behaviour. He was eager to do the will of God and his uncalculated dedication to the highest challenges of the Jewish tradition led to his rejection and death.

I wish to make the case in the following essays that there is no legitimate follower of Jesus apart from this broader perspective of social and political responsibility. The challenges of Matthew 25 are the tasks of all of us who claim the life of this Jewish prophet as our model. Bourgeois Christianity has no place in Catholic life. So why is it so prevalent? Why is it the norm? This is my question. Nor is this for me an academic exercise although I will cite the theologians who support these challenging ideas, or who have helped me to clarify my own perspective.

Since the Second Vatican Council, theologians, priests and laity identified with the task of renewal have often been called liberals because of the value they place on adult moral autonomy vis-à-vis some elements of Church teaching. Those who reacted negatively to these new developments and attitudes were called, also pejoratively, conservatives or reactionaries, implying a lack of theological understanding and/or an inability to leave the secure foothold of an obedient past behind. There are people who enjoy the present conflict in the Church over the values and attitudes that should govern a Christian lifestyle but I am not one of them. I believe that the church is a community where the views of everyone should be welcome, always with the intention of increasing our appreciation for a diversity of viewpoints in a spirit of democratic tolerance and respect.

This reflection on the present and future wellbeing of the church arises from a specific incident but these ideas have been percolating in my mind for more than forty years. The young people who came to adulthood in Canada in the sixties were challenged about the meaning of citizenship by both Pierre Ellliot Trudeau and John Fitzgerald Kennedy. Participatory democracy in Canada and voluntary service at home and abroad were held up as ideals for every young citizen to emulate. I recognize this same moral imperative as a member of the church. I am less interested in whether one is theologically liberal or conservative but more interested in whether being a Catholic involves what a person is going to get – social respectability, moral, religious and personal authority, a career in academia and a community of the cultivated mind, associations of consequence, even an alternative family, aesthetic liturgical experience, etc., or what a person intends to give. If Jesus is indeed the model for our lives, the latter motivation is endless in its demands on our hearts as well as our minds, and has nothing to do with a calculated and self-serving participation.

These interconnected essays are intended to inform the Catholic laity in Canada who have not been part of the theological debates of the last fifty years following Vatican Two. Frequently, educated lay Catholics were deliberately kept in the dark by leaders who underestimated their critical intelligence and emotional capacity for changing ideas. In some cases, it was to protect the authority of the past or a personal clerical or monastic way of living. In some cases it was a lethargic passivity on the part of the laity. I have always found the categories conservative and liberal to be unhelpful when dealing with the Church. I find a different distinction to be more helpful because over a lifetime, I have discovered that it is one's personal motivation that ultimately determines the significance of intellectual truth in the life of a believer, and the subsequent willingness and moral imperative that person feels to honour and sometimes to pay the price of such understanding. This is the question of self-interest. I distinguish between those clergy, religious and laity who come to the Church predominantly for what they can get, and those who come to the Church predominantly for what they can contribute to its quality of life through an informed and active participation in the parish or the diocese, through education and catechesis from elementary school to university, through service to the vulnerable in the community and through social organization of the young in particular.

If people seek out a particular parish for its better preaching and elevated liturgical practice, I certainly understand this need for a refined aesthetics of worship but I believe more is required of the laity than mere ritual observance, attention to a good sermon and financial support. Or even of support for parish activities. In his exquisite poem, *the Four Quartets*, T.S. Eliot reminds us of a traditional measure of the spiritual life, *the purity of intention in the ground of our beseeching*. This has always been an important principle in religious life but I do not believe that this applies only to the professionally religious but to all of us.

The thriving of theological studies since Vatican Two is unprecedented in the history of the church because for the first time, theology is being written by theologically educated religious women as well as men, and by lay men and women who bring different concerns and questions to the table than do priests. The laity possesses a different experience and point of view towards secularism and sexual morality, but also sometimes, a more passionate and engaged interest in issues of distributive justice and poverty, local and abroad. Female theologians, religious and lay, seek to reform androcentric cultures that assume the male experience to be normative for both genders, that often unknowingly perpetuate patriarchal attitudes and other expectations that war against the intellectual, social and political flourishing and emancipation of women. Beyond these internal social issues, this new theological scholarship has rediscovered the centrality of Social Catholicism or what Protestants have called the Social Gospel as a mark of Christian authenticity. As early as the Synod on Justice in the World in 1970, the Catholic bishops of the world declared that a personal and ecclesial commitment to social reform is constitutive of the Gospel, not an option for some but not for others. Never has Catholic theology been so rich, so diverse and so interesting. I write these reflections to encourage the thoughtful lay person to enter into these vigorous debates far beyond the concerns of this introductory volume, and to respond to these challenges in ways appropriate for them.

CHAPTER ONE

Lay Participation Matters: from orthodoxy to orthopraxis

Your heavenly Father knows all that you need...Seek ye first God's reign over you and its justice, and all these things shall be given to you besides. Enough then of worrying about tomorrow. Let tomorrow take care of itself. Today has troubles enough of its own.

Matthew 6:32-34

The issue of what it means to be holy surely is the essence of a Christian life. When I was a young child in Holy Family school in Toronto, we were frequently visited in our classes by Fr. Edward Zeagman, the assistant parish priest and a favourite in the parish, even with adults. Children have a unique ability to distinguish between the authentic and inauthentic, and he was one of the real ones. He told us that we were all called to become holy, to become saints. In that innocent, uncritical pre-Vatican Two world, the stories of the saints were the heroic sagas of our lives. Careful theologians would not use this kind of language and insist that only God can be called holy. Nevertheless, active practising Catholics view moral self-transcendence motivated by God's grace to be central to the significance of their lives. The imitation of Jesus the Christ has a long history in the Church, but is usually associated with Thomas à Kempis, a medieval German writer who exercised a wide influence among priests and nuns until recently. In eastern Christianity, the process of becoming holy is called divinization. In the psychologically sensitized culture of the west, it is argued that the imitation of Christ involves, not a mimicking of the life of Jesus, but rather becoming who we truly are, being true to our highest selves and to our particular callings as they are informed by the values of Jesus, and often by divine invitation.

In 1974, a decade after Vatican Two, the great American ecclesiologist, Avery Dulles, S.J., wrote a landmark analysis of the various communities in the Church, enabling a conversation between these diverse communities and the conflicting ideas and identity that defined them.[1] He distinguished particularly between the charismatic Church and the institutional Church, and viewed the latter as the protector and nurturer of the former. His models, the institutional, the kerygmatic, the sacramental refer to the interior life of the Church. Dulles acknowledges in his fourth model a more recent emphasis on the *church as servant to the world*. Here in my view, he incorporates the demands of Matthew 25, the corrective that Liberation Theology has brought to the Catholic theological world. Before Avery Dulles died on December 12th, 2008, he had added another category, *a community of discipleship,* favoured by Pope John Paul II because it suggests movement forward, like the word pilgrim. Striving for mutual understanding among Catholics committed to one, two or three models to the exclusion of the others, he acknowledges that one's values, and I would add experience, underlie one's preferred choices. I would argue that this fourth category embraces all the others and is non-negotiable, and that it reflects the theological investigation of the last fifty years by our best and most intellectually honest minds. A Christian who lives a life at odds with the values of Jesus may be a decent human being but is not a disciple of Jesus.

The demands of secondary school teaching and administration combined with political activity within my professional association, OECTA and with other groups in the community did not allow me to pursue this issue, though it rankled as I became more and more aware that most Catholic teachers and school leaders had a very limited understanding of the demands of the Gospel in contrast with those of us who had been theologically trained. Hardworking and loyal Catholics, they equated being religious with an upright sexual and family life, observance of the sacraments, especially the Eucharist, and with participating in parish life by teaching Catechism classes or distributing the Eucharist on Sunday. The mark of a genuinely religious person was a kind of sentimental piety expressed through ritual observance. At the centre of their lives, however, were the values of upward social mobility and material acquisition. In this respect, their lives reflected the lives of many clergy. They viewed those of us with a more demanding vision of discipleship as irritating, unreasonable and incomprehensible, and attributed our discomfort with the status quo as a need for personal negative power. Rather, along with so many others from my generation, my personal commitment to social change began during my student days at McGill in the sixties when John F. Kennedy, the civil rights movement in the United States and opposition to the Vietnam War, and in Canada, the justice concerns of the Trudeau era in combination with a growing women's movement, altered the way we thought about our role in society. In Quebec, the Quiet Revolution, especially the anticlerical reaction among French students at the *Université de Montréal* raised questions about the social and economic as well as religious impact of Catholicism on that society. My devout Catholic family from Protestant Toronto where Catholics were often excluded or devalued, found the venom in this reaction of French Canadian Catholics toward the clergy quite shocking and incomprehensible.

In the early nineties, my younger brother Michael, also trained in theology, encouraged me to attend an evening lecture by Roger Haight, S.J. at Regis College in Toronto because this theologian was identified as rather unique within the clerical confines of Catholic seminaries, one with a social Catholic horizon to his thought. In the question period that followed, I asked him what he understood as holiness, if indeed the monastic paradigm no longer served. This brave, intellectually honest man and distinguished scholar looked at me blankly and responded, "Jesus said to call no man holy". Disappointed by what I considered at the time to be an evasion, I realized eventually that as a Jesuit priest living a monastic lifestyle, this was not his question. It was mine. Roger Haight would return to Boston College to write a groundbreaking Christology that has incorporated the recent challenges of liberation and feminist theology, as well as developments in inter-religious dialogue among the world religions.[2] For these attempts to renew and make meaningful the divinity of Jesus, he has been censured by Vatican theologians unwilling to entertain his conclusions that challenge an ethic of monastic civic inaction, an understanding of holiness that is equated with ritual observance, retreats and meditation, and an understanding of the Spirit of God as the force behind other world religions. He turned out to be more pastoral in his concerns, and less dominated by personal emotional needs for institutional acceptance than I had thought. In English Canada, the only noteworthy Catholic theologian addressing this need for a broader and more biblical vision of Christian discipleship was Gregory Baum, and during his time in Toronto until he retired to McGill at the age of 65, he was continually subject to a truly virulent attack from laity and clergy alike. I was often warned about my association with him and his ideas by other priests.

Retirement offered me the leisure to pursue this question in earnest. Why is the social catholic perspective so marginalized in Canadian Catholic society, even in the Catholic school system? I discovered that there is a whole body of Catholic theological literature dating from the seventies that has addressed this same concern. Not only that. These questions date back to nineteenth century European Catholicism when lay voices first came to be heard. Indeed, this is the question at the heart of so many departures from the priesthood and religious life since that time. Ninety-nine per cent of the many former nuns and priests that I worked with in various ways did *not* become committed to social change afterward. They became like other lay people, concerned with professional status, suburban real estate and the demands of family life. In the upper echelons of Catholic school boards, these former religious assumed a posture of moral superiority toward the lay people competing with them for senior administrative positions. They were in fact just like everyone else except they had studied theology and were more sensitive to this critique, although they ignored these biblical demands. Those priests and nuns who understood these historical developments did not communicate them to the laity, although their own spiritual consciousness and practices were altered by them. Protecting their own spiritual superiority vis-vis the laity, conscious or unconscious, is essential to their lives.

The new emphasis on biblical scholarship or exegesis changed the way we measured our discipleship, and the key elements of monastic spirituality came under challenge by the most careful and responsible of Catholic theologians, most of them priests or nuns or former priests and nuns. The concerns that dominate their theology usually reflect whether they are clerical or lay. Priests teaching and writing for the Catholic academy are more apologetic in the original meaning of the word, eager to explain the developments that have occurred in Catholic teaching and defensive or silent about the deficiencies of the past. Lay theologians are concerned with a meaningful dialogue with secularism, modernity and post-modernity, and tend to be more publicly critical. Former priests, like the Irish-American John Dominic Crossan, have focused on the historical context of the life of Jesus, especially his relation to the political dynamics of Palestine during his brief time on this earth. Crossan's competence in this area has made him a regular presence on CNN and ABC but unacceptable as a visiting speaker on many Catholic university campuses. When he spoke at a conference organized by progressive Protestant groups in Niagara Falls, Ontario, I asked him why and he replied, "I am not invited to speak in Baptist or Catholic churches. But I am booked every weekend for the next two years." The question is why.

Since the seventies, the Benedictine nun, Joan Chittester and her associates at Benetvision have made an earnest effort to draw ordinary lay people into an understanding and acceptance of the prophetic reign of God. This was the vision of the ordinary priesthood that the French peritus Yves Congar proposed at Vatican Two. Fr. Michael H. Crosby, a Capuchin Friar from Wisconsin has done the same. Both have left a legacy of compelling reading. These are monastics I admire and trust. They have also been severely attacked for this perspective over the years but mostly they have been greeted with a public ecclesial silence. A willingness to consider these ideas depends more on the heart than the head, and whether one's intellectual concerns, lifestyle or ecclesial career loses or gains through this understanding.

The significance of the life of the historical Jesus in a Jewish socio-political context challenges our understanding of discipleship in an incontrovertible way, and it is easier to shoot the messenger. This perspective emphasizes our consubstantiality with Jesus the man, not Jesus' divine consubstantiality with the Father. It turns out that this is the real question, what was Jesus really saying and why was he crucified by the religious authorities of his day for saying and living it. This is the most divisive issue in the Church today and it underlies the cavernous division within the Catholic theological community. In writing about Jesus of Nazareth, Benedict XVI, an extremely competent theologian, wrote with a very different emphasis than that of other historical researchers in the academic Catholic theological community. Ecclesial authorities have different interests than academic researchers. The truth of what Jesus was about lies first with the biblical and historical scholars. All the other theological disciplines depend on their consensus and conclusions. But the interests and concerns in the life of the biblical scholar also are at play. I have restricted this reflection to the Gospels, especially to the gospel of Matthew, and this illumination of contemporary biblical scholarship underlies every insight.

Rejection and persecution, misunderstanding and tension are usually evidence that a theologian or a person has been faithful to the truth in practice (orthopraxis), and has incarnated a beatitudinal lifestyle that challenges the norm. There is a former nun in Toronto, now reputedly under private vows, who has established a number of houses for political and economic refugees where legal assistance is provided to assist them in their bid to remain in Canada. Never do I hear an admirable word about this woman from priests in the Catholic community. A reductionist criticism of her character is the order of the day. The gospels document this social rejection and persecution of Jesus and then of his community from the response of Herod the Great in the infancy narratives to the growing social alienation of the Jewish Christian community in Syria or Antioch after their expulsion from Judaism. Why were they expelled is the point in question? Was it because they admitted Gentiles to their ranks and were changing the Jewish ritual practices? Or was it because they were trying to be faithful to the vision of Jesus, which was not the normative Jewish religious practice, more focused on ritual than on justice for the poor and powerless.

Prophecy was central to Matthew's spirituality. The prophetic vocation of Jesus and of his disciples was lived within the struggles of human history, not apart from it, in the midst of a society that had hardened its heart to the beatitudinal values of the biblical prophetic tradition. It is a spirituality that must be lived concretely in society in a way that integrates a deepening religious experience with hope-filled prophetic activity. This is the remarkable power and charismatic influence of Barach Obama for whom Christianity represents a bias toward the poor and the powerless, not merely a bid for personal authority and influence. Poverty is condemned in the Scriptures as contrary to the plan of God for human society. The kingdom of God is in the process of being established when the poor have access to the world's resources just like the rest of us. Matthew uses the Greek word *dikaoisyne* seven times in his Gospel (3:15, 5:6,10, 20; 6:1,33, and 21:32) intending the biblical meaning of justice. It is interesting to speculate why this word is often translated as holiness or righteousness meaning liberation from sin rather than given its biblical meaning, God's way of justice or what is now called social justice.

How is it that Catholic parishes are only too happy to organize prayer services and Lentan retreats, and yet no effort is made to mobilize the parishioners on issues of justice except to defend the rights of the unborn child, or to lobby parliament to ensure the continued denial of human rights for the same-sex couple when the legislation was introduced and under debate? Many clergy look to the rich and powerful for their personal validation and social invitations, and the laity, also seeking the reassurance of upward mobility and its status, follow like sheep in this cultural norm. *Do not hunger and thirst for things, but hunger and thirst for justice.* Even in religious orders where evangelical poverty is proclaimed, there is an inordinate interest in the social background of individuals, as if the family's wealth or the father's professional occupation was the defining value of a life. Vows of poverty do not erase these entrenched secular values. And those who truly hunger and thirst for justice in religious life or among the laity are regarded as extremist if harmless fanatics. Yet the great theologian and father of Vatican Two, Yves Congar, called for *all* priests to exercise a prophetic ministry insisting that there is no other kind.

How is it that Catholics believe that justice for everyone is the business of social workers or lawyers or the judiciary, not a central moral obligation of Christian living for everyone, bishops, priests, nuns and laity alike. The answer is that Catholic spirituality is in transition. When the newly elected John Paul II visited America in 1979, he identified the structural barriers to God's plan that exist in affluent societies during a Mass at Yankee Stadium:

> *Within the framework of your national institutions and in cooperation with all your compatriots, you will also want to seek out the structural reasons which foster or cause the different forms of poverty in the world and in your own country so that you can apply the proper remedies ....You will not recoil before the reforms, even profound ones, of attitudes and structures that may prove necessary in order to recreate over and over again the conditions needed by the disadvantaged if they are to have a fresh chance in the hard struggle of life. The poor of the United States and of the world are your brothers and sisters in Christ. You must never be content to leave them just the crumbs of the feast. You must take of your substance and not just of your abundance in order to help them. And you must treat them like guests at your family table.*

Unlike many ecclesial leaders, Karol Wotyla had worked alongside his father as a labourer in occupied Poland, and he understood through this experience the vulnerability of the poor, how social and political cultures fail to take them into consideration when social and political policies are developed by the highly placed and influential. The poor are rendered invisible, or dismissed as the authors of their own demise.

Whatever his other personal failings i.e. his Polish authoritarianism and conservative managerial reform, i.e. the appointment of only conservative bishops and Vatican officials, Pope John Paul II understood the Church's responsibility to speak on behalf of those who had no power, no voice in the public square. He understood how Jesus was challenging the religious norms of his own tradition, and that the values at the centre of his ministry were not limited to ritual observance and sexual morality. In the last years of his life, in failing health, and in league with the Irish rock star, Bono, John Paul II called for the Millenium Year to be a year of Jubilee, a time when the financial institutions of the wealthy western democracies should forgive the crippling debt of the developing world, following the Jewish law. It was the kind of real material debt Jesus was referring to in the *Our Father*, not merely the forgiveness of sins. His secretary for forty years, Cardinal Stanislaw Dziwisz, described in his memoir, *My Life with Karol*, Wotyla's personal contempt for the moral legitimacy of neo-liberalism as a political and economic philosophy.[2] This pope, like his predecessor Paul VI, understood the holistic character of the Gospel, the holistic character of the human body in sexual morality, and the holistic character of the Church's role as an advocate for the world's poor. It is necessary to change one's thought patterns or paradigms but it is not enough. The real task is political, to change the institutional culture so that it reflects these sensitivities and challenges. This will only happen if the laity becomes involved in this struggle for Christian authenticity.

1. Avery Dulles, **Models of the Church,** New York: Doubleday, 1978; more recently Crown Publishing Group, a division of Random House: New York, 2002.

2. Roger Haight, S.J., **Jesus, Symbol of God,** Maryknoll, N.Y.: Orbis Books, 1999.

   The Future of Christology, Continuum International, New York: the Bloomsbury Group, 2007.

3. Stanislaw Dziwisz, Cardinal, **A Life with Karol, My Forty Year Old Friendship with the Man who became Pope,** New York: Doubleday, 2008.

CHAPTER TWO

The Jesus of History and the Christ of Faith

Students in Canadian Catholic secondary schools in their freshman year are introduced to the above Christological categories in the introductory course in Scripture to enable them to understand the life of Jesus in its historical context. These categories, *the Jesus of history* and *the Christ of faith* distinguish between the historical Jesus of the evangelists, already subject to individual interpretation but also shaped by the needs of the communities for whom they were writing, and the post-resurrection experience of Jesus through the Holy Spirit, exemplified most dramatically in the experience of the apostle Paul on the road to Damascus. The purpose of my focus on the historical Jesus is intended to establish Jesus' humanity, his consubstantiality with us, whereas the focus on his divinity is used theologically to establish his divinity, his consubstantiality with God. I am arguing here that an aversion to the historical Jesus in common Catholic practice has sustained a religious practice reduced to prayer, meditation and ritual observance, precisely the kind of Jewish religious practice that Jesus severely denounced in first century Judaism. Emphasis on Jesus' divinity serves to diminish our sense of responsible participation in the challenges of his life and teaching. The Christ of faith is easy. The Jesus of history is another matter. A Christian life that is not historically engaged, that takes no responsibility for the suffering caused by unjust or corrupt cultures in human institutions, that has no appetite for the risk-taking and courage required to confront the injustice caused by human individualism and collective self-interest in society at large is an irrelevant, and I would charge, unorthodox Christian life. At best, it is a mediocre Christian life.

The early historical and theological documents that make up the canonical literature of the Church are primary sources for our understanding of Jesus' teaching. The four gospels are neither biographies nor historical accounts but were probably composed for the liturgical instruction of Jewish Christians. They were written in Greek, the *lingua franca* of the educated, business and ruling classes with sprinklings of Aramaic, the spoken language of Jesus. The gospels represent four different records of the beliefs and collective memory of the early Jewish Christian communities of the first century of Christianity. The shift in the importance now given to understanding the historical and political context in which Jesus lived his mission derives from new emphases raised by developments in historical and biblical scholarship, developments that are shared by Jewish, Protestant and Catholic scholars, and that have altered the way these three religious traditions view one another as well as their own traditions. All of the documents and themes of Vatican Two arose from these new understandings. It is not an exaggeration to say that this new biblical exegesis radically reshaped the Catholic Church's understanding of its responsibility to the world beyond its own institutional confines, and that it continues to challenge the traditional orthodoxy of much later Catholic tradition. Recent decades have witnessed a remarkable output of new knowledge about first century Palestine by archaeological, anthropological, sociological researchers striving to reconstruct the political and economic world that Jesus inhabited.

The influence of Charles Darwin and of the new social sciences in the nineteenth century about the way we interpreted scripture revolutionized the way we understand Jesus as a historical figure, altering church teaching in dramatic and significant ways. Until 1943, this new scholarship was pursued almost entirely by Protestant and Jewish scholars due to its controversial nature, although a small number of Catholic priests/ theologians participated in the research. Over a century or more of many struggles and misrepresentations of this new scholarship, a fundamentalist interpretation of the sacred texts was replaced by a historical and contextual one, but this new method of contextual understanding was not taught in Catholic seminaries and did not take root in Catholic life in North America until after Vatican Two. Albert Schweitzer was one of the most famous of these nineteenth century biblical scholars, producing a landmark study of the historical Jesus in 1905, although his international reputation would be based on his decision to reject such research and take up medicine, knowledge and skills that he took to the African continent. Protestants understood the significance of this decision, that a very able academic had left the study of religion for the practice of it.

This shift in Catholic understanding of how Jesus understood himself and his prophetic call to reform Judaism has created a monumental shift in the evaluation of monastic lifestyles in the Church. Since the nineteen seventies, a biblically grounded critique of forms of religious life defined by prayer and meditation and by a lived social alienation from mainstream society led to many nuns, priests and brothers leaving religious communities precisely for this reason. If the church was indeed to be a *lumen gentium* to the world, to serve the world rather than exist for itself and content itself with its own survival as an institution, but rather to advocate for the poor, a new spirituality was required, one which enabled all Catholics, religious and laity, to become active in secular society, and to put aside the social withdrawal and cultural alienation of the past. Jesus was after all not a monastic but a man of the streets and towns.

Jesus is presented differently in each of the four gospels as the evangelists were writing for specific religious communities with different sensitivities and needs during the last three decades of the first century. Nevertheless, there are constants that appear in all four gospels that constitute the canonical value of these texts for the Church. There is a consensus that the first gospel account by the evangelist Mark highlights a community experiencing persecution about the time of the destruction of the Jerusalem temple in the late sixties of the first century, and the theme of Jesus' persecution and death is dominant in Mark's gospel as an inspiration and reassurance to Jewish Christians. The gospels of Matthew and Luke are constructed using Mark's account as a spine but elaborating Jesus' preaching through a common source of oral tradition referred to as Q. They are called synoptics because they interpret Jesus' life through a common lens, the gospel of Mark and the Q (Quelle) source. The unique Matthean and Lukan additions tell us about the issues confronting the communities Matthew and Luke are writing for. Matthew is addressing the growing Jewish Christian community as more and more Gentiles are admitted into its ranks and as it severs its ties to the Judaism Jesus had originally sought to reform. In Luke's Gospel, the elevated Greek style and language suggests that Luke was a Gentile Christian who had been attracted to and converted to Judaism and was addressing a now predominantly Gentile Christian population. These Gentiles on the fringe of the synagogues were less interested in Jewish ritual than in the ethical commitment of Judaism to the poor. Luke's gospel is a particular appeal to the materially poor, considered to be seventy-five per cent of the population of Palestine at that time, and is not an appeal to the conversion of the rich and powerful. In Luke's Acts of the Apostles, Jesus' followers are called Christians for the first time. John's gospel is very different, more theologically reflective, the last and the least historical of the four, although John confirms the central themes of the three synoptic gospels. I wish to focus on these central themes.

Jesus and the Prophet Isaiah: No Salvation Outside of the Poor

Catholics are familiar with the prophet Isaiah because of the many references to him throughout the Gospels, especially during Advent and the Yuletide season. The book of Isaiah is a compilation of three Jewish authors attempting to capture the complete articulation of Isaiah's prophetic critique of Judaism in the latter part of the eighth century B.C.E. through the reigns of four kings of Judah. As a member of the ruling class, Isaiah exercised an active religious and political role during a turbulent period of Israel's history, excoriating the corruption that had vitiated the conscience of the aristocratic ruling class towards the downtrodden and the poor. Isaiah is the most political of Jewish prophets. He counselled a passive political and military response in the face of an expansionist Assyrian empire, and placed his faith in a temporal salvation that God alone could effect. He condemned the injustice and cruelty of the upper classes toward the insignificant and the powerless. Isaiah was martyred during the reign of Manasseh in the late seventh century by being cut in half with a wooden saw. Twenty-one copies of the entire book of Isaiah were contained in the Dead Sea Scrolls, a cache of 220 biblical scrolls found at Qumran on the northwestern shore of the Dead Sea between 1947 and 1956. This suggests its importance to the Essene community at Qumran. These documents formed part of the library of the Essene community that arose in the second century BCE and is thought to have had an influence on both John the Baptist and Jesus. The Essenes rejected the Temple leadership in Jerusalem as both religiously and politically corrupt, and as a community, they withdrew into an ascetic communal lifestyle in the deserted rocky terrain of the Judean desert, south of Jerusalem. This was a critique of mainstream Judaism that Jesus understood. As everyone knows, he did not join this community, at least not for long.

Centuries before, Isaiah was concerned with the connection between worship and ethical behaviour. He protests the idolatry common at that time, Canaanite fertility rites, including sexual practices forbidden by Jewish law. The theme that underlies his preaching is the establishment of God's kingdom on earth, with rulers and subjects who strive to live by the will of God. Isaiah introduces the theme of the suffering servant whom Yahweh calls to lead the nations but who is horribly abused. This servant of Yahweh will bring justice to earth, a king who brings justice in both royal and prophetic roles. This justice is established neither by proclamation nor by force. Instead the prophet moves quietly and confidently to establish an authentic righteousness in the religious practice of his people, and so that Israel may become a light to the Gentiles. Isaiah prophesies the coming of a Messiah, a person anointed by God in whose kingdom justice and righteousness would reign. Isaiah says of the Suffering Servant that he was sent forth to bring justice to the nations (42:1), to enable the poor, the broken-hearted and the imprisoned to have access to the resources that contribute to the restoration of their dignity. Although he is beaten and abused, Isaiah follows the path that God has called him to without pulling away. His vindication will be left in God's hands. Isaiah came to understand God to be a universal rather than a national or tribal God, a God of all humankind, the only true God who is concerned for the wellbeing of everyone on earth.

Although the gospel texts appeal to other prophets in the Jewish tradition as well, Isaiah has a special place because the political and religious turmoil of his historical period so resembled that of the time of Jesus, a realization probably made in those early Christian communities. When Jesus announces the nature of his mission in the synagogue at Nazareth, Luke tells us he quotes from the prophet Isaiah:

> The spirit of the Lord is upon me;
> therefore he has anointed me.
> He has sent me to bring glad tidings to the poor,
> to proclaim liberty to captives,
> recovery of sight to the blind,
> and release to prisoners.
> *To announce a year of favour from the Lord.....*
> Today this scripture passage is fulfilled in your hearing.
>
> Luke (4:12-21)

The year of favour was the Jubilee Year of Jewish tradition that took place every fifty years, and this Jubilee announced that all financial debts must be forgiven, slaves released from service and the land left fallow for a year to replenish its nutrients. It was a year of both spiritual and economic liberation, a reordering of creation and community. In the *Our Father*, the Greek word *opheilema* signifies precisely a monetary debt, not a spiritual one.[1] Every fifty years, all real debts were forgiven and land that had been lost through indebtedness or expropriation was to be restored. The Jubilee Year began on the Day of Atonement when Jews are required to seek forgiveness from one another for offences committed during the past year. It is a natural thing to forgive the offences of our friends and loved ones. Forgiving monetary debt is another matter. Jesus refers to this in a parable in his treatment of the merciless official, " Then in anger the master handed him over to the torturers until he paid back all that he owed. My heavenly Father will treat you in exactly the same way unless each of you forgives his brother from his heart." (Mt.18:34-4) The miracles Jesus performed were the signs of the Jubilee Year, recovery of sight for the blind, good news for the poor.

In Jewish spirituality, unlike Greek neo-platonic philosophical dualism, there is no separation of the needs of the body as distinct from those of the soul, as each depends on the other. Similarly there is no separation between political and religious life. From the time of Abraham, followed by the liberation from Egypt and the establishment of the kings through the Babylonian captivity and its aftermath, through the Hasmonean uprising and Roman imperialism, the Jews believed that God was in their midst and was concerned for their wellbeing both individually and as a nation on this earth. The story of the Exodus is an emblematic story for all who have fled oppressive circumstances. The Jewish laws that were developed during this period were called *mispatim*. Mispatim is the defence of the weak, the liberation of the oppressed, doing justice on behalf of the poor. This was the intention and original meaning of the legislation. Injustice and oppression were at the heart of the Law and the Prophets. Matthew presents Jesus as the new Moses, as a liberator who has come to deliver his people from the desperate circumstances of their lives, real and psychological as well as spiritual. Jesus made no distinction between the spiritual and the material when it came to people's lives. He had never encountered Greek scholarship and many scholars believe he may even have been illiterate at a time when oral culture dominated life in Palestine except among the learned and the scribes.

The Palestine that Mary birthed Jesus into was an occupied, colonized territory under Roman imperial control. Four legions of Roman soldiers were located in Syrian territory, northeast of Galilee, awaiting any political unrest that might occur.[2] Before his death in 4 B.C.E., Herod the Great had built an elaborate Roman city on the Mediterranean coast, Caesarea, dedicated to Caesar Augustus, and later used by Roman governors such as Pontius Pilate. There would have been a garrison of about 3,000 troops in that location. A despotic egotist, he built other palaces for himself, at Masada on the Dead Sea, the Herodian in the Judean desert southeast of Jerusalem where he was eventually entombed, the Fortress Antonia in Jerusalem and an ambitious extension of the Temple complex there among others. A small contingent of soldiers would have remained in the city through the year, bolstered by troops from the coast during the three major Jewish holidays when thousands of pilgrims would come from all over to attend ritual services at the Temple. In Galilee, Herod the Great used the city of Sepphoris, now under excavation and close to Nazareth, as the centre from which to tax the countryside. These rural peasant farmers were triply taxed: a tithe of ten percent for the support of the Temple and priesthood in Jerusalem, a tribute for the Roman emperor, and local taxes levied by the presiding client-king or governor, Herod Antipas during the time of Jesus' mission. Collectors showed up at the communal threshing floors to claim the king's portion, continually increased to pay for Herod's endless building projects.

After the death of Herod the Great in 4 B.C.E., his kingdom was divided into a tetrarchy, three separate regions ruled by his three sons. Judaea and Samaria were assigned to Herod Archelaus, the eldest; the northern territory to Herod Phillip, and Galilee and Perea on the other side of the Jordan River to Herod Antipas. Approved by Rome for their loyalty and discharged when they proved ineffective, these client-kings were required to keep the public order and to exact the Roman tribute from these conquered peoples. In the rural areas, those unable to pay the burdensome taxes had their properties expropriated, and with the loss of their land as income, they became day labourers living more and more on the economic margin. In 6 C.E, when Jesus would have been close to twelve, an insurrection took place in nearby Sepphoris, led by a popular leader, Judas, whose father had been killed by Herod the Great some years before. These Jewish insurgents took the fortified palace at Sepphoris, armed themselves with the weapons they found there, and seized whatever material goods they could find. Shortly thereafter, the legions arrived from Syria, burned many nearby villages, took the inhabitants as slaves to be sold, and crucified 2,000 men outside the walls of Jerusalem. Antipas rebuilt Sepphoris after the destruction of the uprising and made it his capital city.

Following the pattern of his father, twenty years later Antipas built another Roman Hellenistic city on the shores of Lake Gennesareth (Galilee), this time dedicated to the new emperor, Tiberias. Even this far removed from Jerusalem, the superiority of Roman culture and prestige was encroaching upon the local language and customs of these rural villagers, both fishers and farmers, and was being paid for by their taxes, yet did not benefit their lives. The subsistence farmers were barely able to provide for their families until the next harvest and struggled to pay their taxes. Indebtedness could lead to a loss of their property. As for the fishermen, even in the gospels, there is evidence that the Sea of Genesareth was being overfished, perhaps to feed the growing urban populations of these two cities, or for export elsewhere in the empire.

As Elizabeth Johnson points out, Jesus never mentions Sepphoris, and Tiberias is mentioned only once in the gospels.[2] Perhaps this was because he kept his distance from Antipas who was responsible for the death of John the Baptist. Jesus' attitude toward the wealthy is consistent throughout his public ministry. He distrusts the rich because of what personal wealth does to one's moral compass. He was also a man of the poor, and directed his energies and focus to demonstrating to them that God was present to the material struggles of their lives, and sought their best welfare. He understood the danger that Jerusalem represented for him. That Jesus was a man who cared about the state of their souls but nor for the material wellbeing of their lives, is not only highly unlikely, but from the point of view of a pious Jewish man, religiously heretical and morally barbaric. Johnson speaks of a prophet not as a seer or social critic, but as "someone who participates in the repair of the world". As the Jewish tradition has always asserted, we are made holy by the Spirit of God who leads us to righteous living and acting, not by ritual observance alone. Matthew uses the Greek word *dikaiosyne* to designate both genuine piety before God and moral integrity, and insists that both religious acts, prayer, fasting etc. and ethical deeds be done in private, not to enhance one's social standing.

In the synoptic tradition, Matthew presents Jesus as a charismatic prophet called by God to realize God's righteousness on earth, not to prepare people for heaven, as someone gifted with the power to heal and to cast out evil. Jesus' call to righteousness permeates the gospel, and righteousness takes many forms because it is achieved not by prayer or meditation, as necessary as these are, but by action, not unlike the existentialist claims of the philosophers of the nineteenth and twentieth centuries beginning with Soren Kierkegaard from Denmark. It is important to remember that Jesus is challenging a religious leadership and practice that is focused on ritual observance, and not on the more demanding aspects of the Law. Matthew's presentation of Jesus as one who challenges the conscience and behaviour of the Jewish leadership is interwoven with a series of themes that elucidate God's expectations and designs for the people. Jesus was not crucified because he was a Jewish religious teacher but because he exposed the limited and self-serving interests of the Scribes and the Pharisees, especially their neglect of advocacy for the welfare of their own impoverished countrymen and women with the Roman authorities. He also contrasts his understanding of righteousness with that of John the Baptist whose preaching appears to have focused on repentance and forgiveness. Throughout the gospel there is a tension developing between Jesus' understanding of righteousness and that of other factions. Jesus is identified with Isaiah by the evangelists because he stands in the tradition of the Jewish prophets, but especially of Isaiah in particular.

Nowhere is this clearer than in the Sermon on the Mount, three chapters of instruction in Matthew that begin with the Beatitudes. In Matthew's account, just before Jesus is baptized, John the Baptist condemns the Sadducees and the Pharisees stepping forward for their bath. His language is intense with contempt.

> *You brood of vipers! Who told you to flee from the wrath that is to come. Give some evidence that you mean to reform. Do not pride yourselves on the claim, "Abraham is our father." I tell you, God can raise up children to Abraham from these very stones. Even now the ax is laid to the root of the tree. Every tree that is not fruitful will be cut down and thrown into the fire. I baptize you in water for the sake of reform, but the one that will follow me is more powerful than I. I am not even fit to carry his sandals. He it is who will baptize you in the Holy Spirit and in fire. His winnowing fan is in his hand. He will clear the threshing floor and gather his grain into the barn, but the chaff he will burn in unquenchable fire.*
>
> (Mt. 3: 7-12).

Like the prophet John the Baptist, Jesus will call Israel to justice and righteousness, to return to her prophetic authenticity. When Jesus first instructs the disciples, he sends them to the lost sheep of the house of Abraham, not to the Samaritans or to the Gentiles. Only the resurrected Jesus, the Christ of faith, will enlighten the sense of vocation held by the apostles to reach beyond Israel, to convert all the nations of the earth. And as his mission proceeds, the faith of the outsider, the Magi, the Roman centurion, the Samaritan woman, the Syrian woman will be compared with the lack of faith and deficient moral practice of the religious Jewish leadership.

Later, when the imprisoned John the Baptist sends his disciples to Jesus to ask him if he is the one who is to come, or if they should wait for another, Jesus replies,

> *Go back and report to John what you see and hear: the blind recover their sight, cripples walk, lepers are cured, the deaf hear, dead men are raised to life, and the poor have the good news preached to them. Blest is the man who finds no stumbling block in me. Mt. 11:4-6.*

Unlike John, for whom repentance and forgiveness were central in his mission, Jesus makes no mention of this. Later he will say that the last person in the kingdom of God is greater than John the Baptist.(Mt.11:11) Jesus' emphasis on the need to forgive the injuries of others in Matthew 18:21-2 is immediately followed by the parable of the unforgiving debtor, a parable that it not about the forgiveness of sins but about the forgiveness of real material debts. The kingdom of God is a utopian metaphor for the world that God has envisioned for those who seek to realize God's plan for humankind while living on this earth.

The author of the Gospel of Matthew was writing to support a community in transition, a community being rejected by the Pharisees at Jamnia in Syria as an illegitimate expression of orthodox Judaism. Their official expulsion from Judaism has been dated to ca. 88 C.E. Matthew has been characterized as a Christian scribe who presided over the liturgy and was a teacher of both adults and children in the synagogue, interpreting the texts and helping to reconcile Jesus' teaching with the Jewish prophetic tradition. Matthew's community was dealing with persecution from within its own Jewish religious communion, and trying to find its own identity as a Jewish community committed to the values of Jesus who saw himself in the prophetic tradition. This period in Judaism was enlivened by a wisdom spirituality, the later Jewish texts still referred to as the wisdom literature, and Matthew's gospel is sometimes called the book of Wisdom. Jesus appeals to this tradition to clarify what he considered to be the heart of Jewish teaching – God's partiality for the poor, the divine reversal. *The last shall be first and the first shall be last.* Drawing on the words of Second Isaiah in his inaugural address in the synagogue at Nazareth, the constant in his appreciation of his evangelical mission was the need for everyone to right the injustice afflicting his poor and suffering people.[3]

From 63 BCE, Palestine had been invaded by Roman imperial interests that were expropriating their land and emptying their waters of fish. Twice in the Beatitudes, Jesus blesses those who struggle for God's righteousness. The reign of God in the Jewish tradition proposed a world where God's plan for creation was recognized and realized, a world where the dignity and flourishing of each man and woman is honoured and supported, where resources are shared and indebtedness periodically forgiven to provide for such a quality of life. The Sermon on the Mount, beginning with the Beatitudes, is focused on the characteristics of God's reign as Jesus presented them. The miracles announce the power of God's presence when faith is exercised in their midst and the parables describe the perils and process of conversion required to become a part of the reign of God. The Last Judgment just before the Passion summarizes again what behaviours are required. Once again there is no reference to the primacy of ritual observance or to the primacy of the forgiveness of sins in Jesus' understanding.

Matthew presents Jesus in the three chapters of the Sermon on the Mount as the great teacher like Moses, called by God to liberate his people and to demand of them a greater righteousness than ritual observance, prayer and meditation. The beatitudes present the divine inversion of God's values, that God's values are not ours.

> *How happy are the poor in spirit. Happy the gentle. Happy those who mourn. Happy those who hunger and thirst*

> *for what is right. Happy are the merciful. Happy are the pure in heart. Happy the peacemakers, Happy those who are persecuted in the cause of right. Happy are you when people abuse you and persecute you and speak all kinds of calumny against you ....this is how they persecuted the prophets before you. Mt. 5:1-12.*

In the above translation taken from the New Jerusalem Bible where Christian biblical scholars worked closely with their Jewish counterparts, righteousness is translated as *what is right* or the *cause of right*. In the French Douay-Rheims translation, the simple term *justice* is used. In the New American and Ronald Knox translations, *tzedek*, the Hebrew word for righteousness is translated as holiness, not *what is right* or *justice*. The correct translation of the words is important. To be righteous in the Jewish tradition means many things - to be upright, just, straight, innocent, true, sincere. Jesus also identifies righteousness with obedience to the divine plan, an obedience identified as a gift of grace. With this richness of meaning, righteousness is a key motif in the Gospel of Matthew.

> *Set your hearts on his kingdom first and his righteousness and all these other things will be given to you as well. Mt. 6:33.*

> *Wisdom is proven righteous by the things it does. Mt. 11:19*

> *Someone who deliberately misleads other people can never be called righteous. Mt. 12:38*

Righteousness is a quality of God that must become engrained in our moral consciousness.

The demands of ethical righteousness are further elaborated in the *You have heard it said,.....but I say to you* sequence. Jesus is creating a heightened appreciation of the claims of the Jewish law, clarifying and refining its meanings for interior dispositions but also for action, for a more exemplary practice, a greater fidelity to the expectations of the Creator of the universe. Jesus addresses a number of moral issues: the importance of one's word, caution about judging others, adultery and divorce, radical giving and genuine prayer, authentic discipleship... It is a call to a higher compassion, a more radical love, a more private purity of heart. The disciple's actions must reflect an interior communion with God, not a demand for social affirmation or recognition. Those who are persecuted for righteousness' sake must pray for those that persecute them, must love their enemies. Formal religious observance or status in the community is not mentioned. Observance of the Sabbath, the dietary obligations, tithing, almsgiving were fundamental to Jewish life but they did not reflect or imitate the heart of the law, the righteousness of God. The authentic disciple is not the one who prays and meditates but the one who does the will of his Father in heaven.(7:21). Jesus gives the Lord's prayer to illustrate what we are about.

> Our Father Who art in heaven,
> Hallowed be thy name,
>
> *Thy kingdom come,*
> *Thy will be done on earth as it is in heaven.*

This call is followed by the assurance of God's tender nurture in our lives, our daily bread, forgiveness of indebtedness and deliverance from the evil one.[4]

Remember where your treasure is, there will your heart be also. Jesus speaks about the treasures that we harbour in our lives. Treasures command the heart, the centre of our lives, and may function as a competing allegiance to one's desire to please God. The treasures of God compete with the treasures of this world. The blessings outlined in the Beatitudes in the gospels of Matthew and Luke are not what we normally associate with treasure. The first beatitude, *Blessed are the poor in spirit* in Matthew becomes in Luke, *Blessed are you poor*. Some scholars have suggested that Matthew was writing for a more affluent community than Luke, and so he focused on *spiritual* poverty. Poverty of spirit is a traditional biblical theme, emphasizing a complete and absolute trust in God's care and an unqualified willingness to submit to God's specific will for our lives. (Ex. 22:25-27; 23:11;Lev. 19:9-10; Deut. 15:7-11) Trust in God's providence allows us to make the realization of the kingdom on earth the centre of *our* lives. Luke's statement, *Blessed are you poor,* the central motif of Luke/Acts, is a direct salutation as he is addressing the poor in the community. He is making the case that the poor are closest to God's heart, not because they are deserving but simply because they are poor.

This statement should never be interpreted as an endorsement of poverty as a good thing. Real poverty is never life enhancing, but denigrating and destructive, crippling the imagination and the possibilities of life, an offence to human dignity and self-respect. Only those who have all their material and spiritual needs met and who live lives far removed from those who struggle to provide food and shelter for themselves and for their families would utter such foolishness. It is not enough to choose a simplicity of lifestyle for one's own spiritual benefit. Those who choose a simple, non-materialistic lifestyle in imitation of Jesus are obligated to struggle to improve the lives of those who are truly poor. Simplicity of lifestyle is not enough if it serves only one's own spiritual wellbeing, one's own salvation. Later Jesus will challenge the rich young man to leave his possessions behind and to join Jesus' band of nobodies to seek a greater good than personal wealth and the power and status attached to it, a life dedicated to the realization of God's reign on earth. He is unable to do this because he has defined his personal value according to the treasures of this world.

When the church developed under Constantine as an imperial institution after the fourth century of the first millennium, the demands of the Sermon on the Mount were directed to monastics, men and women living in religious orders or congregations, and to those individuals who did not have to face the compromises of public life. The medieval Italian saint, Francis of Assisi particularly represents this uncompromising biblical spirit. *But Jesus does not address these words to a particular group.* All disciples are called to these norms, regardless of lifestyle, both clergy and laity. In contemporary language, we exist to make this world a more humane, a more loving, a more inclusive, just and empowering place. We exist to become the moral salt and religious light for this world, to become a church community that is truly a *lumen gentium* in a world often scarred by darkness and despair. The humanistic Christianity that is advanced through Catholic educational institutions and parishes is not enough. Christianity is not merely about personal cultivation. Jesus' entire sermon contrasts the behaviour of those who put Jesus teachings about the demands of God's reign into practice and those who do not. The internal dynamic between Jesus and the Jewish leadership was his active compassion and engagement with people and the remote apathy and disengagement of their separate reality. The spirituality of Matthew's Gospel is this call to active engagement on behalf of others. *Woe to you scribes and Pharisees. Hypocrites! You pay tithes on mint and herbs and seeds while neglecting the weightier matters of the Law - justice and mercy and good faith. It is these you should have practiced, without neglecting the others.* (Mt. 23:23).

Blessed are the pure of heart. Purity of heart is the ongoing desire to live in God's presence, and to be worthy of God's presence by reflecting his radical love in the actions of our daily lives. This total commitment to God's plan for the world through this personal call in our lives is reflected in righteous deeds. Purity of heart is also the ability to see and to hear what is important, what truly matters, and to discriminate against the trivial and the superficial. Wisdom, the presence of the Spirit in our lives, helps us to understand what truly matters. As we learn to internalize the values of God, the trivial values so dominant in the culture and reflected everywhere through the media, the endless identification of personal worth with consumer power, the addiction to appearances and narcissistic display, the middle class obsession with respectability, upward mobility and social status, wither in the power they exercise over our lives. We begin to see and to hear with the eyes and ears of God. "*No one can serve two masters. S(he) will either hate the one and serve the other, or be attentive to one and despise the other. You cannot give yourself to God and money.*"

Blessed are those persecuted for justice' sake, the reign of God is theirs. The last beatitude proposes that those who incarnate the beatitudes as Jesus did will provoke the conscience of those who do not. Rejection and slander and persecution will be the concrete signs of this fidelity. *Blest are you when men insult you and persecute you and utter all kinds of calumny against you because of me. Be glad and rejoice, for your reward is great in heaven; they persecuted the prophets before you in the same way." Mt. 5:10-12.* The experience of persecution, misunderstanding, tension with the larger community marked the community that Matthew was writing for. He speaks of Jesus teaching in *their* synagogues (4:23) suggesting that

Jewish Christians were already forming separate communities of worship and lifestyle outside. Perhaps in Antioch or somewhere else in Syria, it becomes clear that they are now celebrating their own rituals, a baptism for all nations, (28:19), the Eucharist, (26:26-29), and have rejected the dietary regulations, (15:11, 17-18) and Pharisaic teaching in general. (15:12-14;16:5-12) In the latest and least historical of the gospels, John has Jesus give this warning: *If you find that the world hates you, know that it has hated me before you. If you belonged to the world, it would love you as its own. The reason that it hates you is that you do not belong to the world. John 15:18-20.*

Jesus does not encourage anyone to abandon the world for the sake of personal purification or personal salvation, for angelism or pietism. He means that we must divest ourselves of the way the world interprets reality, of the values that it acknowledges and rewards. Discipleship is different from the pursuit for worldly success and the fulfilment of our ambitions. *Do not suppose that my mission on earth is to spread peace. My mission is to spread not peace but division. I have come to set a man at odds with his father, a daughter at odds with her mother, a daughter-in-law with her mother-in-law; in short to make a person's enemies those of her own household. (Mt. 10:32-35)* As Jesus prepares the disciples to promote the kingdom of God in the towns and villages of Galilee, to preach, to perform miracles and exorcisms, he also prepares them for rejection. Fidelity to the promotion of justice, constitutively linked with God's reign, exacts a price, because of the challenge it presents to those locked in narrower forms of religious expression and who cling to a smaller horizon of morality. *"Whoever loves father or mother, son or daughter more than me is not worthy of me. He who will not take up his cross and come after me, is not worthy of me. He who seeks only himself brings himself to ruin, whereas he who brings himself to nought for me, will discover who he is.(10:34:39)*

To do God's will is equated with resistance to the will of this world's powers and principalities because it is truly against their will. Jesus began to teach them that they would be rejected by the chief priests and the scribes because their hearts were hardened and they would not recognize the deeds of Jesus' life as an expression of God's justice (Mt.8:31). True knowledge consists in fidelity to God's creative plan, not to one of one's own making. In describing the indifference of the Jewish leadership, Matthew insists *that the stone the builders rejected has become the keystone of the structure. It was the Lord who did this and we find it marvellous to behold. For this reason, I tell you, the kingdom of God will be taken away from you and given to a nation that will yield a rich harvest. (Mt. 21:42-43)*

This is a demanding discipleship, not a Christianity of the comfortable pew. Mark also tells us that Jesus understood the enormous challenge to Jewish religious practice that he had unleashed, and indicates that this teaching will bring the rejection of the elders, of the chief priests and of the scribes (Mk.8:31). John tells us that they could not recognize God's justice in Jesus because their deeds were evil, and they lived in darkness. (Jn.3:17) *I have told you all this, Jesus warned, to keep your faith from being shaken. Not only will they expel you from the synagogues. A time will come when anyone who puts you to death will claim to be serving God. All this they will do to you because they knew neither the Father nor me. (John 16:13).*

In Matthew, Jesus' life exemplified the Jewish wisdom teachings of the period. True wisdom consists in fidelity to God's plan for the world, not for one's personal advance or authority. Jesus' prophetic spirit took him beyond angelism and pietism, beyond legalism and authoritarian control, beyond hierarchical privilege and exclusivity, and eventually beyond religious sectarianism and nationalism. The chief priests were aware that the crowds recognized Jesus as a prophet and feared that his arrest would provoke reaction (Mt. 21:45-6). He was put to death precisely because he lived the teaching he proclaimed. Matthew presents Jesus as a prophet rejected for his prophetic lifestyle. Those committed to justifying the self-centredness and venality of their lives will always condemn those whose motivation they neither understand nor value. The refusal of conversion maintains the status quo, a hardened conscience the refusal to change.

> *Listen as you will, you shall not understand.*
> *Look intently as you will, you shall not see.*
> *Sluggish indeed are these peoples' hearts.*
>
> (*Isaiah 6:9-10; Mt. 13:13-17*).

In the last judgment scene, the specific acts of mercy reflect the classical biblical and Jewish categories of care for those in need: food for the hungry, drink for the thirsty, welcome to strangers, clothing for the naked, care for the sick. Twice earlier, Matthew presents Jesus performing miracles to feed the hungry. (Mt. 14:13-21;15:32-39). Just after Christmas in 2008 in the Saguenay region of Quebec in the midst of a global economic downturn, a mother and father made a pact to kill themselves and their children after his business had failed and he had declared bankruptcy for the third time. Such desperation and despair is about real hunger, the inability to care for one's own children. I do not think Jesus would have spiritualized their need to suit his own availability.

> This rather is the fasting that I wish:
> Releasing those bound unjustly, untying the thongs of the yoke;
> Setting free the oppressed, breaking every yoke;
> Sharing your bread with the hungry,
> Sheltering the oppressed and the homeless;
> Clothing the naked when you see them,
> and not turning your back on your own.....
> If you remove from your midst oppression ,
> false accusations and malicious speech;
> If you bestow your bread on the hungry
> and satisfy the afflicted.
> Then light shall rise to you in the darkness
> and the gloom shall become for you like midday.
> Then the Lord will guide you always and give you plenty,
> even on the parched land.
> He will renew your strength
> And you shall be as a watered garden,
> Like a spring whose water never fails. (Isaiah 58:6-12)

In biblical times, almsgiving was a moral social responsibility for everyone, even the poor. In the late nineteenth century as republican democracy was taking hold in the various countries of middle and southern Europe, lay Catholics moved beyond the adequacy of charity and almsgiving to meet the challenging conditions of poverty and social degradation in the lives of the working classes, and made a commitment to transformational social justice, to political action in order to change legislation by forming organizations to support the working poor in their desire for a decent and dignified existence on this earth. In our advanced democratic societies, care for these people is often addressed through appropriate educational expectation, social policy and support services that some political candidates and political parties encourage and others do not. This does not excuse the need for a personal response to poverty and distress as well, but a collective governmental response, often motivated by local grass roots activity, is the most effective means of social reform in modern democratic societies. Economic rights to employment, to housing, to medical care have become the measure of a civilized society.

Jesus concludes the beatitudes with the images of salt and light, images of daring, strength, endurance and ethical example presented as qualities of righteousness, and then he outlines the demands of those who would enter the kingdom of heaven. Authentic disciples provoke reaction but also enlighten the world about what God wants for all of his creation. They do not settle for business as usual or the cocoon of bourgeois comfort.

> *Do not imagine that I have come to abolish the law and the prophets. I have come not to abolish but to complete them. ....For I tell you that if your virtue goes no deeper than that of the scribes and Pharisees, you will never get into the kingdom of heaven. Mt. 5:13-17.*

Because Jewish tradition discourages any direct reference to God's name, heaven in this case did not refer to afterlife as was understood for so many centuries in the Catholic church, but to the reign of God here on earth, to those aspects of life on earth where God's values rule and take precedence, to the values of God being expressed in personal, social and political behaviour.

Rarely do preachers address this question of the plan of God for creation. I have always listened carefully when they did. There is usually an assumption that the congregation already understands. I used to interpret this as God's call to me, the particular calls of my own life as the years passed, i.e. my experience of the Holy Spirit guiding the significant decisions and directions of my life. I was retired with much time to read theology before I was presented with the understanding that God's plan for creation, from my local community to the outreaches of the international community, is a plan of justice, of righteousness for all, so that all may live in dignity, their bodies clothed and fed and housed, their minds exercised through educational possibility, their lives emotionally rich and fulfilled. God's reign is far more significant than my personal salvation and it is not only spiritual. God cares for the whole person, not just for his or her spirit. And it is a communitarian salvation, the salvation of everyone, a social salvation, not just for Christians. Jesus sought to be faithful to the plan of God, not to the plan of Caiaphas. He did not come to die for the sins of humanity but to liberate humanity from the consequences of sin, to fulfil God's plan for history. Theories about salvation reflect the theological locus of the interpreter. If the interpreter has personally opted out of a concern for transformational justice, is it surprising that a reductionist concern with personal salvation persists, focused on the moral peccadillos of one's limited life, even if this interpretation is not biblically grounded. Those who exist only to tend to their own salvation, or to serve the salvation only of the members of the ecclesia, do not often hunger and thirst for extra-ecclesial righteousness. They are nothing more than the blind leading the blind.

Often the will of God is interpreted as observance of the norms of personal Christian morality that too many Catholics still equate with sexual morality. As we enter into the life of God, we become responsible for reflecting God's values, for becoming salt and light and revealing God's creative intent for all of us in His creation. God is larger than the parish or the Catholic Church or all of Christendom. He cares as much about the African animist child or the Chinese communist leader as he does about any of us who consciously engage in the religious practice of Christian ethics, personal, interpersonal and social. God's plan for our individual life is larger than us, just as our lives are larger than ourselves. God enters our lives in order that we may reflect his will in our own existential life decisions. In loving and accepting us unconditionally, so must we love and accept others. But this gift of grace is not just for us. God seeks the wellbeing, the salvation of everyone and the Gospels witness to how Jesus, in imitation of Isaiah and of the prophetic tradition of Israel, has revealed how this elevation of human dignity and worth is at the heart of God's intention for all of creation.

> *Bring no more worthless offerings; your incense is loathsome to me.*
> *New moon and Sabbath, calling of assemblies, octaves of wickedness:*
> *this I cannot bear.*
> *Your new moons and festivals I detest; they weigh me down, I tire of the load.*
> *When you spread out your hands, I close my eyes to you.*
> *Though you pray the more, I will not listen....*
> *Make justice your aim. Redress the wronged. Hear the orphan's plea. Defend the widow.* (Isaiah 1:2-17).

The Spirit of God is a spirit of empowerment, of nurture, of relationship, of empathic and compassionate response, of magnanimous and wasteful generosity, especially toward the nobodies of this world. There is nothing of control or dominance or repression or criticism in this Spirit. It is a Spirit of Life, of positive energy and confident support so that everyone may flourish and have enough, but especially the nobodies. Worthiness is not a condition of God's attention, nor gender, nor social position, nor educational degrees. Christianity is a participatory democracy where God's presence is available to everyone, not to a select few who have been ordained in a patriarchal tradition determined to protect its own religious and social privilege, or to the kind of lay passivity and self-absorption that these entrenched interests silently endorse. Jesus calls us to evolve beyond adolescent expressions of religion to an adult consciousness of what is true and of what is false religious living, to an adult empowerment that changes the world and that empowers others rather than, in an hierarchical reflex, reducing them to an inferior classification, the collective behavioural norm of an authoritarian culture. God enters into our history to recognize us in our unique circumstances, and to liberate us in myriad ways, empowering us toward self-realization so that we may contribute to the empowerment and flourishing of others. This is not a patronizing form of care like charity. The recognition of another's talent, the creation of new opportunity or possibility is an expression of God's justice.

As the Jewish Christian community for whom Matthew was writing began to appreciate during the last decade of the first century that Judaism would not accept the teaching of Jesus, would not be transformed as a community, the liturgical practices and attitudes toward Judaism would change as more and more Gentiles entered the community but the central focus of Jesus' teaching would not. The later evangelists interpreted the destruction of the second Temple by Rome in 69-70 C.E. as an expression of God's judgement for Judaism's rejection of Jesus and of his community of table fellowship then still very much a Jewish affair. Only gradually, as is evidenced in The Acts of the Apostles, will these communities begin to see themselves as a group apart and come to call themselves Christians. The condemnations of the Pharisees would become in John's Gospel, the condemnation of the Jews, texts that would be used in later centuries to justify xenophobic European anti-Semitism leading to social discrimination and then to pogroms and to the Holocaust. But when they were written, they expressed the disappointment and growing alienation of Jewish Christians toward Judaism itself. As the Jews were driven out of Israel by the Romans and settled in the north, disinherited of their own land until 1948, the Pharisees took charge and it is thought that the orthodox patterns of Judaism became more rigidly defined.

Themes of physical danger and social rejection pervade Matthew's account, beginning with the slaughter of the innocents in the infancy narrative demanded by Herod the Great, through the capture and death of John the Baptist by Herod Antipas to the humiliation and crucifixion of Jesus. Neither of these Jewish prophets was murdered because they were preaching religious heresy or advancing an ethic of the afterlife. They were both critical voices, and their voices were silenced because they spoke the truth about the corruption of the Temple. In the last days in Jerusalem, Jesus was not condemning the moneychangers per se but the Temple leadership that equated observance of the Law with ritual sacrifice, and the material profits and comfortable lifestyle that issued from this self-serving religious practice.

In the parables, Jesus addresses the suffering and injustice afflicting the lives of his countrymen and women because of Roman exploitation and Jewish religious compromise and quietism. The politics of emperor worship and the economics of imperial exploitation impacted the lives of the upper class of religiously observant Jews and the rural peasant majority differently. Jesus advocated for the latter group because he came from them and understood the suffering of their lives. The Temple leadership remained silent in the face of the Roman dominators, eager to preserve their power, influence, wealth, authority, control and privileged social standing, and as a group, they justified their silence as necessary for the protection of their institutional interests and perpetuation. As a Roman citizen himself, Paul's concern was to temper the response of these Roman/Jewish authorities toward the young Christian communities, struggling to find direction and to remain faithful to Jesus' teaching, and yet even Paul, so concerned to accommodate Roman power, insists, " *The kingdom of God is not a matter of eating and drinking but of justice, peace, and the joy that is given by the Holy Spirit."* (Rom. 14:17).

Christianity is not just a personalist religious faith untouched by an effective, informed, energetic engagement with the powers and principalities of this world that deny economic and political rights, employment, educational opportunity, to so many people with whom the middle class do not associate. A moral Christian life that is defined by a narrow self-interest is not a Christian life, however commonplace among the clergy or of some people in the parish. The Church itself is always subject to the biblical critique and never above it. The opinion of the rich and powerful, or even of the smug middle class, is not the measure of its orthodoxy. When the acceptable norm of parish life has become an introverted community of mutual self-interest for spiritual growth and moral support, it is, for lack of leadership, no longer a community of Christian disciples. And the serious ones, the Christians seeking to reflect the concerns of God expressed by the Crucified One become exiles in their own Church, offended by the mediocrity of its religious practice and moral indifference to the evil in the community beyond the Church walls, as the leadership settles for a passive acceptance of the status quo.

Unlike many Jewish leaders, Jesus was killed because he was unable to retreat into a false consciousness about the betrayal of the officially religious towards their own people. Eleven of the twelve apostles died violent deaths for the same reason. These Christian leaders were not militarists or political zealots, but Jewish Christians living in fidelity to the moral and religious perspective Jesus had illuminated and drawn them into. They did not retreat into an ecclesial world of refined culture and career ambition. This is the meaning of the cross, not the ordinary struggles and challenges of our lives, however consuming and exhausting these may be from time to time. In Jesus' time, the cross was a symbol of political insurrection, not of innocent suffering or self-mortification. The cross is the price Christians pay for seeking the truth of who God is and for pursuing single-heartedly and uncompromisingly the righteousness of God in their families, workplaces, neighbourhoods, cities, country etc. They do not spend their lives in prayer and meditation although these practices may be part of their daily routine. Jesus was killed by the Jewish leadership in league with the imperialist power because he exposed the truth of who they were, and of how they had betrayed the heart of the Law, the heart of God.

In the collection of the Art Gallery of Ontario there hangs a large painting of Jesus as the *Liberating Christ*, painted by Fred Varley and dated to 1934. My question remains, why has this Christological principle been absent until recently from the Catholic conscience? The name of Jesus, Yeshua or Joshua, recalling the ancient Jewish leader who led his people into the promised land, means *Yahweh saves* or *Yahweh is Liberator*. The child of Mary is called Yeshua/Jesus because he will liberate his people. When God calls us by name, he is calling us out of our anonymity into a life lived for others and we become co-liberators with Jesus showing us how to become effective instruments for God's creative purposes.

Naming one's reality, as Adam demonstrates in Genesis, is to enter into the creative purpose of God. To be stripped of that potential as has been the case of the laity, including the women in the Church, is to be stripped of this participation in God's creative intent. Distributive justice, not retributive justice, exemplifies God's justice. The forgiveness of sins is not an expression of divine power but an expression of divine compassion, a new acceptance of self, a new beginning, a new future of expectation and hope in one's life. Distributive justice is what follows, a commitment of the Christian disciple to the realization of God's creative intention for the world, that all may share in the fullness of life, especially those most disadvantaged by the accident of birth. No one is exempt, at least in the mind of God. Jesus castigated the scribes and Pharisees with their norms and traditions because they nullified God's word *in favour of the traditions you have handed on. (Mt. 7:13)* They disregard the heart of the Law in favour of a religion defined by institutional self-interest, by their own collective needs reinforced by the necessary theological justification. In Romans 1:25, Paul alleges that they have exchanged the truth for a lie.

1. Michael H. Crosby, O.F.M., Cap., ***Thy Will Be done, Praying the Our Father as Subversive Activity,*** Orbis, Maryknoll, N.Y., 1977. p.p. 117-135 (chapter 7)

2. John Dominic Crossan with Jonathan Reed, **Excavating Jesus; Beneath the Stones, Behind the Texts,** Harper:San Francisco, 2003.

3. Elizabeth A. Johnson, C.S.J., **Consider Jesus, Waves of Renewal in Christology,** Crossroad, N.Y., 1990.

4. Michael H. Crosby, **Spirituality of the Beatitudes,** pp. 3-11. Orbis Books, Maryknoll, N.Y., 1981

5. Michael H. Crosby, *Thy Will Be Done, Praying the Our Father as Subversive Activity,* op.cit, pp.136-162.

Further Reading:

Marcus J. Borg, ***Conflict, Holiness, and Politics in the Teaching of Jesus,*** Trinity Press International: Harrisburg, Penn., 1984.

CHAPTER THREE

Pro-life and Anti-life Religious Consciousness

The cult of sacrifice is anchored in the powerful language of belief. The cult needs the mysteries of faith and the promise of afterlife to encourage this devaluation of the present, of the here and now. Channelling sexual desire away from life is an important process in the creation of the death cult. Erotic energies are harnessed. Sexual phobias are fed by distorted theology or spirituality. Fear and loathing of women, mixed with anxiety about one's own sexuality is a potent combination.

Michael Ignatieff, *The Lesser Evil*

These lines are taken from Michael Ignatieff's examination of the psychology required to create a political Islamic terrorist. Young men are persuaded by trusted religious elders to sacrifice their often tedious and meaningless lives to obtain some personal significance by acts that deliberately target the lives of innocent civilians to create an atmosphere of chaos and terror in the community. Ignatieff spent the nineties as a journalist covering genocidal conflicts for the BBC and other media, notably Saddam Hussein's attack on the Kurds in northern Iraq, then the disintegration of the former Yugoslavia into ethnic, religious and regional enclaves where local militias joined established armed forces to take or protect territory. Christianity was not a primary factor in these conflicts, and so he is not writing about Catholic cultural influences. He has written both fictional and non-fictional accounts of these nationalistic and ethnic political conflicts, and sought to comprehend what cultural and ideological convictions could lead people to slaughter their former neighbours in order to take their land. He touches on a riveting insight into the political nihilism that drives our present international politics.

Michael Ignatieff is the son of a former Russian count George Ignatieff, who was educated at Lower Canada College and Trinity College at the University of Toronto, became a distinguished Canadian diplomat to Yugoslavia, to the United Nations where he served as president of the Security Council, to NATO, and who, in retirement, became the chancellor of the University of Toronto. Russian Orthodox by birth, Michael Ignatieff was a student leader at the University of Toronto in the nineteen sixties when student power was at its apex, and I voted for him and for his friend, Bob Rae as they became the first students elected by the student body to represent their peers on the university's board of governors.

The first time I heard Michael Ignatieff speak publicly years later, he declared from the pulpit of Bloor Street United Church that he was not a religious believer but an agnostic. Only in the United Church of Canada would a non-believer be invited to preach on Sunday on the nature of moral consciousness. His later writings established his credentials as a thoughtful and grounded philosophical liberal, but recently his books have addressed the evil of ethnic hatred and terrorist affiliation. In *The Lesser Evil*, he explores the mind, the ideology and the socio-religious context of the suicide bomber, of the terrorist who seeks meaning for his life by losing it in order to achieve some kind of victorious dominance in various kinds of ideological political conflicts.[1] Ignatieff begins in nineteenth century Russia with the repeated assassination attempts made against a politically progressive Tsar, Alexander II after he had abolished serfdom and had encouraged the Russian peasants to become independent by purchasing their own land in order to improve the quality of their families' life. A determined social reformer, Alexander II was assassinated by a member of a radical leftwing group in 1881.

Not long ago ten locations in Mumbai were invaded, bombed, set on fire, and infiltrated by unknown terrorist Islamic groups looking for foreigners– two five star hotels, the train station, a bar frequented by backpackers, a hospital for women and children, a Jewish enclave, to name a few. The citizens of this city of nineteen million people were panicked and normal life was in disarray. After twenty-fours hours, heavily armed commandos were still travelling from floor to floor, clearing the hotels of these armed fanatics. The civilian death toll reached 171, including two Canadians and five Americans, with over 300 wounded. Unlike the western secular democracies, developing societies continue to be deeply religious and religious ideas and ideology are powerful motivating forces. Before strapping on their body explosives, and taking up their weapons, these young men spent the night in prayer, and shaved the hair from all over their bodies to purify themselves according to the rituals of their particular affiliation to reassure themselves that they were doing God's will and would be appropriately rewarded after death. How is it that religious beliefs can be used to serve death and destruction, instead of life and liberation?

Michael Ignatieff has never been interested in Roman Catholicism, and he makes no reference to Christianity in this analysis. The question he raises, however, is a theological one. In the New or Second Testament, Jesus identifies himself with Life and sees his own role as a giver of abundant life marked by an uncalculated generosity, healing body and soul, bringing into his community the excluded and the insignificant, liberating people from the burdens of their past destructive behaviour, and from the oppressive poverty of their lives. And yet the Catholics of my pre-Vatican Two generation always identified Jesus with the Cross. A young man asked me the other day in a shop when I mentioned that Advent was upon us, why did the priests wear purple? He was not a Catholic but I could tell that he was a gay man. He was not being impertinent. He was trying to understand something. Why is it that Catholic priests don purple vestments, signifying a formal liturgical period for penance and mortification when the rest of the world is enjoying the festivities of the holiday season. Even if the

Catholic laity are enjoying themselves at their various Christmas parties, many feel that they should not be. Now I do not mind if the clergy prefer to spend the four weeks leading up to Christmas giving up their treats and mortifying their flesh, but do not call this the will of God. Although many of us rejoiced some time ago when the Canadian episcopacy focused its attention on the issue of Bread for the World, a noted Catholic theologian was heard to comment, "I only hope they do not do to bread what they have done to sexuality." God did not put us on this earth for deprivation and self-denial. He came to give us abundant life. And he expects us to invite everyone to the banquet, to the table of plenty so that all may eat and drink and flourish.

I was always surprised when, a young thing in my twenties, I went to study theology and was repeatedly confronted by the assumption, first by priests, and then by Catholic lay men, that I was running away from my sexuality and that this evasion was at the heart of my obsession with God and Christian service. In truth, I was not the least bit afraid of sex from what I had experienced of it. I was, however, deathly afraid of living a meaningless life in some suburban domestic backwater with a man whose goals and aspirations were unworthy, and who represented for me a lifetime of secure but intolerable boredom. There is so much hypocrisy on this issue of sexuality among the clergy, homosexual and heterosexual priests alike, in religious orders and in dioceses, that a laywoman who does not marry is now highly suspect. Indeed, my professional reputation was scarred by this cynical and pervasive suspicion among married laymen and women, especially ex-religious, gay and straight, in Catholic educational circles, that my attempts at denial became futile, their certitude was so unshakeable.

I had also realized that those who equated a religious vocation with some kind of social status, educational ambition, power and significance within the Catholic community if nowhere else, would never comprehend the life of someone governed by other motivations, who fully realized the price she would pay for taking up theology not only in a secular culture but also in her own Catholic professional and ecclesial milieu. Nonetheless, the presence of large numbers of gay men and women in Catholic religious orders is no longer denied or maintained in silence. There is some validity to the cynicism I encountered. Monastic orders and communities have become a refuge for gay Catholics from a world still hostile to their orientation, though secular life is less in denial about their prevalence and their emotional needs than the official Catholic Church, and more supportive of the public legislation required to recognize their legitimate human rights. Personally I do not care, as long as the norms these communities choose to impose on their own members are not claimed as a higher holiness for the rest of us to emulate.

The rejection of a sexual life can occur for many reasons. Often the seeds for this derive from the family of origin, from parental relationships or attitudes, or from a disillusionment with the nature of family life. One priest actually admitted to me that he did not want the bother of a woman. Many spoke of their homosexuality. Even in secular society, men and women seek alternatives to the family lives they have experienced. Religious life offers other possibilities, lives of committed service to others, high culture and educational achievement, significant recognition at least in the Catholic community. As a Catholic laywoman, I have personally benefited from the awareness and support of many nuns and priests over the years, and I do not discredit their lives. I do however discredit a spirituality that eschews secular society, and confuses its own spiritual and material poverty with a religious ideology and practical lifestyle that devalues participation in the good life of this world, the world I was created to serve. This is a deformed interpretation of Jesus' intent, of his teaching and living, however useful it might be to encourage a life of service to the Church.

In an unexpectedly candid way, when Jacqueline Bouvier Kennedy asked her devout Catholic brother-in-law Sargent Shriver to arrange the funeral details for her husband's public funeral, she made the observation that the one thing the Roman Catholic Church was good at was death. More recently, a C.B.C. news show, *The Sunday Edition,* not the usual hardcore secular critique when it comes to Catholic matters, reported how a community of monks in Canada was constructing coffins to survive economically. How far we have come from the daily production and relishing of earthly things by medieval Benedictines and Carthusians. Not cheese or wine or liqueur, but coffins. If ever there was a symbol of contemporary monastic spirituality, still elevated as its touchstone of personal holiness by the Catholic hierarchy, recently by Benedict XVI, it is the coffin.

All the great world religions except Judaism include monastic traditions-especially Hinduism, and the various forms of Buddhism. If monastic spirituality was not elevated as a higher form of Christian life, if it was truthfully regarded for what it is, a departure from the Gospel tradition to provide refuge for those unable or unwilling to address the evils of society with a legitimate Christian orthopraxis, necessary for some but hardly normative for the rest of us, I would not be engaging in this polemic. Catholics need moral leadership from their bishops and priests, a moral leadership that is not limited to abortion, same sex marriage and stem cell research, but that uses its authority to advocate for justice and to transform the economic, cultural and material conditions that adumbrate the fullness of life for so many of their fellow citizens, Catholics and otherwise. Charitable appeals, largely to benefit church organizations, appease the conscience of the comfortable but do not address the sources of poverty and alienation. And it is insufficient for these concerns to be occasionally addressed by the Canadian Conference of Catholic Bishops but never mentioned or acted upon at the parish level.

God created men and women to flourish on this earth, to share in all of its physical, sensual and cultural beauty, to live lives filled with meaning and to share their excess of social respectability and wealth with those on the margin, to contribute toward the betterment of our social institutions and political life. Charitable giving is not the same as discipleship. It is what we do with our lives that matters. Sallie McFague, an American feminist theologian has commented: "Tell me what you do with your day and I will tell you what your theology is." Moral leadership involves a broadly informed moral passion for the good life that everyone is entitled to participate in, and the parish is the place where these concerns should be discussed, debated and acted upon in concert. Think of the social and political impact Catholic people would have on their communities if priests did not restrict their concerns to the state of their buildings, and to what goes on in the bedrooms of their gay and heterosexual parishioners. From the point of view of the Gospel, this is the scandal. Not Catholic politicians unwilling to impose their own Catholic moral standards on everyone else in our pluralistic and democratic society. The silent indifference of the episcopacy and of priests to the daily issues that diminish the real lived lives of people, an indifference justified by a collective understanding of priesthood reduced to ritual, homilies and aesthetics, this is the scandal that originates in an anti-evangelical spirituality that advises the laity to light a candle and to pray for the victims of evil. This was the solution recommended by the pastor of a university parish in Toronto after the events of 9/11. He was very intelligent and theologically progressive, but he was governed in his own life by the monastic spirituality and clerical norms of his Basilian order.

The laity, probably because they bring children into the world, and seek their welfare and wellbeing in that world, view life differently than the professionally religious. In the latter part of the nineteenth century in France, Belgium, Italy, Switzerland and Germany, Catholic lay aristocrats began to gather in study groups with interested clergy to develop a concerted ecclesial response to the "social question". The new liberal, industrial capitalism was being constructed by entrepreneurs indifferent to the working and living conditions of the *popular classes,* and justice demanded that those with social power speak out and address these conditions. Leo XIII published an encyclical, *Rerum Novarum,* a first of its kind to respond to this exploitation of the politically and socially powerless working poor in 1891. Leo XIII was himself from an Italian aristocratic family, but he had a personal history of advocacy on behalf of the socially and politically powerless from the time he was a young bishop, though he was a royalist, an academic and essentially conservative. The encyclical was a response to thousands of French workers who travelled to Rome every September on pilgrimage from the late eighteen eighties, each year their numbers doubling, and seeking the support of the papacy in their struggles

The document was drafted by a layman and expressed the moderate consensus that had developed at the Fribourg Union to promote labour associations informed by Christian values, to encourage state intervention to achieve a twelve hour workday in a six day week, to eliminate child labour, and to provide for the worker's safety in the workplace and a pension when he retired. This was the birth of Social Catholicism. Fifty years after Marx had published his Manifesto, his moral outrage and the ideas issuing from it had become commonplace, had informed the democratically elected leaders as well as the legislative decisions of the Paris Commune, and, while the Church clung to the privileges of the *ancien regime* that ensured its income and social standing, its moral authority continued to corrode in the minds of the labouring population.

Though a monarchist himself, a year after Rerum Novarum, in a second letter to French Catholics alone, Leo XIII encouraged the people to stop opposing the Republican ideal and to enter into the political life of France, a pragmatic political decision that nonetheless had many wealthy and devout Catholic women praying for the pope's early demise. But a distrust of the democratic exercise of power continues to be embedded in clerical consciousness, despite reams of theological treatises being written in graduate schools on the *sensus fidelium* of the laity and the legitimacy this holds, even in canon law. Yet the hierarchy continues to decide what is best for everyone, continues to reject a democratic faith in and for its own people and refuses to acknowledge the possibility of their spiritual equality and concerned judicious participation in ecclesial decision-making. Such a church is a social anachronism. It seems to be enough for the clergy that the laity should pay the bills, bring their children to the sacraments, and defer to episcopal authority, even when there is no evidence of the collegial consensus announced as legitimate canonical procedure at Vatican Two.

Although John Paul II was an authoritarian and patriarchal man, a true son of his native Polish culture, a leader inimical to the redistribution of power within the Church even among the episcopacy, he had one powerful redeeming element in his personal history. He had performed physical labour alongside his father when he was a young man, and he had a heart for those who worked hard for a living. *Laborem Exercens*, his encyclical on labour, was provoked by the nationalist liberationist goals of the Solidarity Movement in Poland and his desire to support these brave souls trying to free Poland from the Russian hegemony controlling their civic and economic lives. The encyclical addressed, among other things, a philosophy of work as essential to the development of human personhood, the limits of totalitarian socialist and democratic capitalist systems, and the social responsibility of employers, even in difficult economic times towards the people they employ. This stirring and prescient document that he wrote himself, as modern popes are inclined to do, became a signpost for incipient democratic nations especially in Eastern Europe and South

America, but also in other parts of the developing world where labour and human rights have not been enculturated, even if they have been legislated. It is legitimate to ask how the local Churches have supported these ethical values that so influence the quality of life of the lay people in the pews.

In the Catholic schools of Ontario there are few nuns left. In Toronto, the Basilian priests and Christian brothers have privatized their schools to focus on the children of the Catholic elite. Until recently, all of these schools were managed by fiscally responsible religious men and women who gave their professional and personal lives to the maintenance and expansion of these institutions. However this is no longer the case. In Canada, even before the sexual scandals, Catholic families no longer encouraged their children to enter religious communities, as parental admiration for these vocations has dramatically diminished. In Toronto, the leadership of these communities have come to accept that they are part of a dying lifestyle. The question has become focused on who will care to maintain these educational and medical institutions in the future, whether there is the political will to protect them, and whether the Christianity being promoted through the culture of these schools is any different from the addictive consumerism and obsession with real estate, status and the various kinds of prestige of secular life in secular public schools.

If monastic spirituality is no longer appropriate for the laity, who will operate these schools and will a biblically informed spirituality permeate the culture? I favour the radical, demanding, intellectually informed spirituality of those French laymen and women in Paris at the beginning of the twentieth century who disdained the conservative social values and privilege of their parents and Church to reorder French society so that the rights of workers and of the marginalized poor would be recognized, first by the political culture, and then in parliament through legislated change. As the search for the historical Jesus was underway in Protestant scholarly circles, a new appreciation, a new reverence for human life in this world was shifting Christian spirituality in a more biblically oriented direction. The Magnificat of Mary announcing the divine reversal, Jesus' inaugural declaration of the meaning of his ministry in the synagogue in Nazareth as he repeats the words of Second Isaiah, the Beatitudes and the Sermon on the Mount present Jesus in the prophetic tradition of Judaism, seeking to promote the values of God, not the values of the ecclesiastical compromise of Temple and Empire that prevailed in Palestine, and, if contemporary historical scholarship has gotten it right, that was intensifying the poverty and desperation of the peasant class. Jesus was obedient to God, not to Caiaphas. We need to inquire how this challenging, achingly biblical, socially engaged, non-dualist existence became in Catholic life a spiritualized pursuit of life after death, with all the life-denying behaviours that derive from such a spiritual worldview.

1. Michael Ignatieff, *The Lesser Evil, Political Ethics in an Age of Terror,* Princeton University Press: Princeton, N.J., 2006.

CHAPTER FOUR

The Dysfunction of Monastic Spirituality

I was one of those young Catholics who loved everything about monasticism, and personally identified with the Catholic medieval tradition and mystics beginning with St. Benedict and the broad influence of his Rule. I reflected on the life of the mystic Julian of Norwich, loved especially the emphasis on prayer and contemplation, was intoxicated with nostalgia for a time when chivalry and gallantry were highly espoused virtues, and admired the focus of the monasteries on hospitality and on learning, as they represented the early beginnings of public schools. The Trappist monk Thomas Merton was an influential figure during the nineteen sixties when I attended McGill University in Montreal, and a small group of Catholic students met every Tuesday night at a young American's digs to discuss Merton's writings, especially his spiritual journals i.e. *Seeds of Contemplation*. A former Jesuit seminarian, James McElligott was a doctoral student in psychology but also my first experience of someone seeking to be part of the NASA space program.

Organized by the chaplain at the Newman Centre, we spent an annual retreat after exams in May at St. Benoit du Lac, a Benedictine monastery on the shores of Lake Memphramagog in the eastern Townships. Every fall, students from all the French universities in the province, with small groups from the English universities of Ottawa and McGill met for a weekend on pilgrimage, climbing Mt. Orford on the Saturday, and on Sunday walking the ten miles from the town of Magog to St. Benoit du Lac for the final solemn mass. The monastery is located on rising hills overlooking Lake Memphramagog and in the autumn with the trees ablaze with colour, the entire French Canadian countryside of this region is uniquely beautiful.

Thomas Merton was a convert to Catholicism during the forties, influenced by Catherine Doherty, the Baroness de Hueck, and Dorothy Day, lay Catholics who had opened houses of hospitality for the poor in New York City, the former in Harlem, the latter on Delancey Street in the Bowery on the Lower East Side. These women represented social Catholicism on this side of the Atlantic. Merton entered the Trappist monastery of Our Lady of Gethsemane in Kentucky at a time when this expression of monastic life was commonly considered the most challenging of all in Catholic life. By the fifties, Thomas Merton had become a public literary figure, recognized for his poetry as well as spiritual writings. *The Seven Story Mountain,* his spiritual autobiography, became a best seller and I read it at my brother's suggestion while in high school. Merton recovered in his writings the historical luminaries of monasticism, major and minor, especially Bernard of Clairvaux, John of the Cross, and many others. As evidenced in his journals, he corresponded with literary figures in England, France, South America and his own country, and was clearly aware of international politics and literary culture in the world beyond the Church. He provided my reading material in spirituality for years.

In the mid-sixties living alone in the woods on the property of his monastery, he was challenged in correspondence by the lay Catholic historian and theologian, Rosemary Radford Reuther, always direct and honest, this time about the inappropriate values he was advancing for the laity through the persuasiveness of his talent. He began to write about an ecumenical dialogue then taking place among the monasteries of the great world religions, about the evils of racism and war and poverty, themes that began to dominate his retreats to religious men and women, ideas recounted especially in his last books, *Reflections of a Guilty Bystander,* and *The Asian Journal.* He writes of exchanges he had in meetings with

Hindu and Tibetan monks, and recounts his meeting with the Dalai Lama. He died in India, on December 10th, 1968, killed in a freak accident when an electric fan fell across his bed. In biographies written about him, it is clear that in those last years, he fell in love with his attending nurse during a period of hospitalization for stomach ulcers, and attempted to leave the order to marry. These attempts were frustrated by his superiors as he had become internationally known by then, and a source of financial as well as influential benefit to the Trappist community. He died as this process was unfolding.

For those of us who had come under his spiritual influence, these developments of his thought during the activist sixties were revealing. It would be many years later, however, before I came to realize the significance of this transformation in his way of viewing spirituality, especially after Vatican Two as the church had once again begun to see itself as a public advocate for the poor of the world. Ideals are important because they shape our lives, even when they represent a false consciousness that is perpetuated by those whose interests they serve. This critical assessment of the negative impact of monastic spirituality on the lives of Catholics would never be written by someone still committed to the monastic lifestyle, and the traditions that support it. I write these lines as a committed Catholic laywoman because I must.

It should be sufficient to say that Jesus was not a monk, and unlike the monastic community of the Essenes in the desert south of Jerusalem that seems to have shaped his perspective, Jesus was always a man of the streets and of the towns. He never advocated a life lived apart from the mainstream, or a religious practice absent of service to the socially vulnerable, to the sick and to the poor. He was murdered by Jewish priests of the Temple in Jerusalem aligned with the imperial power of Rome because he challenged the corrupt distortion of orthodox Judaism that they represented. His was an undeniably political life, although he was not, like the Zealots, a revolutionary political figure willing to use violence to remove the imperial power from the land. The political and the religious were intertwined in first century Palestine, and we must not view the period through the perspective of separation of Church and State bred of our post-Enlightenment understanding. Rome was eager to impose its own religious values, gods and goddesses celebrating the family unit, and peace and harmony throughout the empire. Men like Pontius Pilate who attempted to force this acceptance soon discovered that the Jewish people were not eager to embrace this religious option, and he seems to have settled for a détente in the matter.

It should be sufficient to say that Jesus was not a monk but it is not. In a religious culture dedicated to the imitation of Christ, the Catholic Church of North America seems to favour the sweetness of the Christ of Faith over the demanding discipleship of the Jesus of History. I am asking that we return to an ecclesiology that truly is a *lumen gentium* to the world, a *lumen gentium* that celebrates God's love for the world and the fullness of life that the Creator intended for everyone, a personal flourishing and quality of life that the Church itself is willing to fight for at the local level, to advocate as an expression of God's justice. Secular life must not be measured against a reduced experience of life adopted in religious communities, by those who have fled the secular city but not necessarily its destructive obsessions with status and endless personal recognition. Mostly, we must stop measuring the lives of ordinary lay people against the norms of monastic spirituality, of celibate, clerical life with its distrust of sexuality, its rejection of secularity, and most ashamedly as we witnessed in the support of the American episcopacy for the Republican Party during the historic election of Barack Obama, its preferential option for the rich and the powerful because they support its conservative sexual teaching.

Monastic behaviours can be found in all religious traditions, in Islam, in Hinduism and in its own reformist movement, Buddhism. Usually originating with individuals who have fled mainstream society for lives of isolation and prayer, the historical pattern is that communities of like-minded individuals come together, and engage in behaviours of self-abnegation and asceticism combined with prayer and meditation. The early hermits lived in isolation and liturgy as we know it was not available to them. Gradually they began to live together and various practices evolved. In Roman Catholicism, Benedict of Nursia created such a community ca. 529 at Monte Cassino in Italy, and founded another dozen independent monasteries in his lifetime. The Rule of St. Benedict became the norm for subsequent religious orders and communities until the twelfth century.

The Dominicans and the Franciscans founded in the thirteenth centuries were attempts to reform traditional monasticism and to make it more responsive to the needs of the Church and of the world: the Dominicans to improve the quality of theological instruction and preaching, the Franciscans to address the needs of the poor and of social outcasts. It is not the monastic religious order that is at the centre of this critique, but the primacy of its spirituality in the life of the Church, even among diocesan priests, bishops and popes.

In contrast with usual assumptions about monks and nuns, it may be that the laity are not only more effective in their evangelization, but less inclined to be drawn into the communal behaviours that religious orders and communities often produce- a pettiness of character issuing from a pattern of people living very small lives, a relentless and competitive careerism that is all-consuming but described as *mission*, an anti-evangelical individualism and self-centredness that belies the claims about the significance and purposes of community life, and an attitude of derisive psychological reductionism toward those in their own communities who actually serve the poor and the unimportant, and resist the communal norm of the order. Even the most selfish of parents gradually learns over time to put aside his or her interests so that the needs of children may be addressed. These are empirical observations gathered over a lifetime, not gleaned from a few months of association. And these conclusions were arrived at with considerable sadness and disappointment, from concern with the truth, not from malice. While the moral and spiritual development of lay people is often curbed and rendered mediocre by the married and social partnerships they have entered into, the normative behaviour in religious communities can also be marked by a surprising mediocrity that may have its source in the collective psychological personality of a community, as well as by the values, overt and covert, that govern that psychological norm.

Just as the concerns of priests and parish teams rarely transcend the interests of the parish, so do the collective and individual concerns of religious rarely transcend the needs and concerns of the religious order.

After six Jesuits and members of their staff were murdered by political extremists in San Salvador, a call went out to Jesuits all over the world to replace them. A talented Canadian Jesuit was chosen. When he returned to Canada, I asked him what was the most important thing that had happened to him during his years in El Salvador. He surprised me by saying his participation in a national conference for his fellow Jesuits *in Canada*. He did not reference at all his experience in Central America. While mission statements refer to service to the larger community, in practice this refers to the community of the religious order or of the Church, and except for sisters working in city hospitals or prisons, rarely to the world beyond itself. While this unfortunate intra-ecclesial culture may be widespread, men and women come together in these associations to address personal needs for familial relationship and religious support, and this is perfectly legitimate. What is not legitimate is for anyone to elevate these norms to a status of holiness to be emulated by the laity. Many of these professed religious have a great deal to learn from the laity about real self-sacrifice, real altruistic and generous living. Monastic living is simply one choice among many to serve God's will in a world racked by injustice and dehumanization.

In the end, it is not the fact of religious communities that function in their social isolationism within the Church that is at the heart of this critique. People can live this way if they need to or wish to. What must be remembered is that monastic living is contrary to the biblical values of Jesus who did not give his life to prayer and contemplation but to the service of other human beings, especially those in various kinds of pain, physical, psychological, social, material and spiritual. Prayer and contemplation were essential to his generous altruism and he prayed alone, usually in the early morning hours. Nor was his an academic lifestyle. His life was not defined by a personal need for ever-increasing status in the church or in the educational world. Educational institutions require well-educated teachers and managerial leadership to provide Christian leaders in service to the world, but they also serve the interests of the Church and often do not reflect biblical values in their internal communal cultures. Due to poor instruction, many students graduate from Catholic institutions with no sense of the Church's responsibility for social transformation, and understand only an ethic of charitable giving, not evil in itself but hardly evangelical, and entirely inappropriate in mature democracies where participation in the political process is key. Often the clergy and nuns who run these institutions see only the social distinction or dollars that former graduates can bring to the institutions they manage, and do not appreciate the scandal that these often less than subtle attitudes convey. The members of one religious order in Toronto are famous for seeing only what the laity has to offer financially.

Any spirituality that devalues this present life and the social responsibility of the Catholic community to improve the quality of life of society as a whole is anti-evangelical, and cannot be justified as exemplary, regardless of how long it has persisted in the history of the Church. That the lives of the laity should be shaped and governed by these assumptions – that true Christian living is about prayer and contemplation, ritual and aesthetics, withdrawal from society and communitarian safety is a travesty of the life of Jesus. Had he remained in the desert, fasting and praying, he would never have provoked the reaction of the Temple leaders and of their political associates as he did, and he would have otherwise lived a long if solitary life. Matthew documents the condemnations of the Pharisees, the lay liberal theologians of their day, and of the Sadducees, the aristocratic traditionalist priests and landowners who constituted the country's financial and social elite, for their tendency to say the right things while living from other concerns. As has been stated earlier, Matthew was writing after the uprising against the Romans and the destruction of the Temple in 70 C.E. at a time when the Jewish leadership, now reduced to the Pharisees at Jamnia, were less tolerant of diverse practices and becoming hostile toward Jewish Christians who were admitting to their ranks Gentile converts and transforming the internal practices of their community, although there is evidence in the Gospel that the Jewish rites, dietary practices, tithing etc. were still being observed by Christian Jews if not by Gentiles. Matthew presents Jesus as a man obsessed with justice not ritual, with service to the weak and insignificant and unhealthy, and to those too unclean to be part of the religious community.

Jesus had come, he said, not to abolish but to fulfil or restore the Law and the prophets, the heart of the prophetic tradition, and he outlines these values and demands in the Sermon on the Mount. These demanding criteria of true discipleship are interwoven throughout the miracles and the parables, and find their starkest demonstration in the scene of the last judgment in Matthew 25. There is no mention of social upward mobility, career accomplishment or the pursuit of ecclesiastical office, but a repeated emphasis on service to the poor, the outcast, the social undesirables, and of the divine justice that governs this predilection of God for the least of these. Nor does Jesus distinguish between the deserving and undeserving poor when he insists that this kind of service takes precedence over sacrifice and other aspects of liturgy. The prophetic tradition of Judaism was alive in Jesus' teaching and in his practice. It was not an option for a few but a criterion of authenticity for the lives of every person of faith. The former Archbishop of Milan, Carlo Cardinal Martini, Jesuit trained, theologically progressive, the author of more than forty books, acknowledged in a paper that he published after his retirement that he had spent his life escaping from the demands of Matthew 25. Open to the ordination of women, to a rethinking of traditional sexual morality, a strong supporter of Catholic schools and of action on behalf of immigrants and refugees, he was more honest than most.

The biblical theme of justice central to the Jewish Testament provides the underpinning of Jesus' ministry in Matthew. From Jesus' announcement of the nature of his ministry in the synagogue in Nazareth, taken from the prophet Isaiah, through the Beatitudes and the Sermon on the Mount, to Jesus' description of his mission in distinction to that of John the Baptist when John send his disciples to Jesus, through the miracles and parables, to the scene of the last judgment, the issue is always *orthopraxis*. What are you doing for the least of these? This central focus is accompanied by the realization, first by Jesus and then by the Christian community after his death, that it is not the lost sheep of the children of Israel and their leadership who have responded to Jesus' mission in faith, but the non-Jews - the Magi, the Roman centurion, the Samaritan and Syrian women, and later the Gentiles, and these will replace the Jews in the Christian story. This is the symbolism of the fig tree that does not bear fruit and is later cut down by Jesus. *Not those who say,"Lord,Lord", but those who do the will of my father in heaven.... I have come not to abolish the law or the prophets but to fulfil them.* The justice of God is not limited to the forgiveness of sins, the spirituality of John the Baptist, but embraces all of human existence, all of human life. Christian life for everyone, clergy and laity alike, involves more than prayer and contemplation. Everyone who is loved by God is obligated to actively improve the quality of life of others whoever they might be, not just advance their spiritual or career development, and to encourage the human flourishing of others as well as one's own.

Matthew addresses this issue of those who refuse to be converted to God's plan for the world. Jesus says, " I use parables when I speak to them, because they look but do not see, they listen but do not hear or understand. Isaiah's prophecy is fulfilled in them.

> Listen as you will, you shall not understand,
> Look intently as you will, you shall not see.
> Sluggish indeed is this people's heart.
> They have scarcely heard with their ears,
> They have firmly closed their eyes,
> Otherwise they might see with their eyes,
> And hear with their ears,
> And understand with their hearts,
> And turn back to me and I shall heal them."
>
> Mt.13:13-17; cf. Isa. 6:9-10

Isaiah concludes by describing the consequences of prophetic ministry, the reaction of a society hardened to beatitudinal values and resistant to conversion. Jesus' prophetic spirituality is not about nourishing one's faith only, but must be lived concretely in society in a way that integrates a deepening religious experience with hope-filled prophetic activity. The response to the transcendent experience of God in the Spirit is an acute and concrete awareness of sin, both personal and societal.

This was the critique of post-enlightenment existentialism toward an oppressively authoritarian and ethically quietistic European Christianity. In existentialist ethics, using the categories of Thomas Aquinas, a life of moral *becoming* is integral to the quality of a person's *being*. Prayer and contemplation are not enough. A willingness to sacrifice on behalf of the common good is essential to a prophetic spirituality. Yves Congar's insistence on a prophetic priesthood for everyone with no exceptions was influenced by the changed consciousness of the social Catholic laity and priests in France and elsewhere in Europe who refused to follow a leadership indifferent to *the social question* then dominating the secular public conscience. Today the Catholic churches of Paris are divided by an intransigent clerical rejection of this perspective, entrenched in a defensive pre-Vatican Two ritualism or institutionalism, and those identified with an open evangelical spirit of service to the community. It usually depends on the socio-economic standing of the community. According to the prophetic ministry of Jesus, however, charismatic activity cannot be separated from a commitment to justice in the world. A selective or deliberate inattention to the demands of the beatitudes is simply not on.

> I, the Lord, have called you for the victory of justice.
> I have grasped you by the hand;
> I formed you and set you as a covenant of the people,
> *a light for the nations.* Isaiah 42:6.

The concept of obedience is obedience to the divine will and to the values of Jesus first. Jesus brought together into community a diverse collection of largely insignificant people and insisted that they live the beatitudes, not merely proclaim them. Jesus did not merely proclaim the "acceptable year of the Lord". He outlined in his associations and activities the path to be taken to accomplish it. The prophetic reign of God is in the process of being established when the poor have access to the world's resources through a this-worldly struggle by everyone including the poor to ensure a just distribution of this world's goods until everyone's basic needs are met.

The clearest expression of this prophetic spirituality has come from the poorest regions of the globe, from the Catholic theologians and bishops of Central and South America, Africa, and Asia, especially Sri Lanka and the Philippines, where the impact of poverty is so widespread and unavoidable. The domestication of Christianity in a Church that served the upper and middle classes and where the poor were absent has been challenged by a popular movement of the people supported by the biblical leadership of nuns, priests and lay catechists living and evangelizing in the barrios, favellas and slums, presenting a liberating God through the prophetic ministry of Jesus. Centuries of religious quietism have been challenged by the realization of the poor that God cares for their material as well as their spiritual wellbeing, and that God's empowering spirit is with them in their demands for social justice – employment opportunity, just wages, good public schools, decent housing and the public availability of electricity and clean water and the hygienic elimination of human waste. A Christianity devoid of concern for the material needs of the people would be inhumane and unthinkable. Just as modern science has claimed that justice is part of our human DNA, God's plan for creation is inseparable from justice and the flourishing of the entire human community.

Nonetheless, liberation theology has been divisive, usually along the interests of social class, and Protestant evangelicals have swept into these countries by emphasizing religious experience alone, reinforcing this proclivity for an emphasis on spiritual needs alone. The upper classes prefer traditional forms of piety, spiritual retreats, liturgical devotions etc., because they find these new biblical challenges disturbing, and are inclined to resist and devalue them. A traditional focus on acts of charity is easier than a commitment to transformative public justice. The conservative conventions of the past brought harmony and peace to their lives, not conflict and the need to take sides. Monastic indifference to the injustice of the world becomes the *new* orthodoxy

It must be said that a deformed and clericalized theology and years of adumbrated spiritual formation in seminaries and convents have legitimated a focus on personal rather than on social sin, on spiritualized interpretations of salvation, freedom from sin rather than freedom from oppression and injustice. The liberation theologians have had their theology and their lives scrutinized by official Roman theologians with little pastoral commitment to the faithful of the world beyond their own role as defenders of the authority of the Church. The sexual sins of the faithful are much easier to address than the denigrating material and psychological conditions of their damaged and impoverished lives.

There has been no lack of papal documents however. Paul VI in a general audience in 1973, addressed the need to reshape the Catholic conscience and lifestyle through critical reflection on the part of our ecclesial institutions, and he recognized the need for both an intellectual conversion and a renewal of heart. In the seventies and early eighties, the Canadian bishops published annual statements addressing this more critical stance toward the status quo, citing various regional and global issues like the exploitation of native lands for oil exploration in the MacKenzie Delta and hunger at home and abroad. These continue although without the same determined regularity. Sadly, these documents are rarely mentioned at the parish level, and continue to be a secret for the majority of the Canadian laity.

Spirituality has to do with the way we feel sustained by the Spirit of God, by Mary, by Jesus and by the saints of our history. Spirituality speaks to an eschatological hope in the midst of human struggle and darkness and organizes our lives around transcendence. Self-transcendence as moral development is not unique to the religious conscience. Those who demand moral excellence for themselves look for similar aspirations in others, and regard those who settle for personal moral mediocrity in religious or secular communities with disappointment, or sometimes a dismissive contempt. The prophets, before and after Jesus, and the saints who followed him in the course of history, set this higher moral norm in the context of a religious conviction. We are all of us called to be attentive to these voices in our history and in contemporary life. The exercise of moral courage in difficult secular contexts is not the same as an obsessive, private perfectionism because it comes from the magnanimity of the heart, not from a narrow spiritual self-absorption.

Through the prayer of discernment and through poverty of spirit, what the French call *disponibilité*, we enter into the wisdom of God and leave our own wisdom behind. Exclusivism, elitism, hierarchical separation, these are the values of humankind, not the values of God. Civil religion, the incentive to personal success in its myriad forms, conspicuous consumption, trading up in the spheres of influence, is fundamentally anti-evangelical. God does not measure our lives by these values. If the leadership culture of the Church endorses this civil religion, these commonplaces idolatries, they obscure through their silence or moral mediocrity the voice of God. God promises to be with us to meet our most essential needs, yet we seek security in our own resources. Learning to trust in God's providence takes time and practice.

> *Seek first this reign over you, God's way of holiness, and all these things you've running after will be given to you besides. Mt. 6:33.*

Our spirituality must root itself in God's providence, in the specific promises that define our lives. This inner peace is God's gift to us, allaying our anxiety and concern for the future.

It is not however for ourselves alone. The new creation to which we are called is the reallocation of the world's resources, where economic and human rights are recognized by market forces and government intervention. The Lord of History calls everyone to be active in this task, to a worldly holiness in the midst of the forces of darkness, not to be hiding from them. We must strive to be faithful to God's revealing presence in our lives, seeking to realize his will rather than serving the gods of traditions that have abandoned the world to serve the idolatry of personal salvation.

When a church community uses a selective reading of Scripture to justify a reprehensible silence in the face of evil and injustice, that community has abandoned the divine will for some other religious idolatry, an intransigent worship of past practice and an adumbrated spirituality that Jesus would have disowned. Democracies were formed to address the rights and needs for human sustenance that the powerful land-owning aristocracies claimed only for themselves. As Christians we are called to be obedient to the agenda of God, not to a collective agenda of personal advancement, academic display and ritual observance, a travesty of Jesus' mission and of the discipleship to which we are called. As Peter declared in the Acts, "Better for us to obey God than men." (5:29). A gospel of peace only has validity if it is based on justice, not on a quietistic, disengaged and self-serving religious individualism. The Passover meal signifies a passing over from oppression to liberation in the fullest meaning of these words. In Matthew's judgment scene, there is no reference to ritual observance or to miracles or to prophecy. God recognizes those who in their ministry of justice, enable the hungry, the homeless, the imprisoned, the ill to have access to the resources that they need. Matthew is claiming that to be known by God, we must ensure that the just needs of these are addressed. Participation in God's liberating presence in history is the only condition of authenticity. Paul chastises the community for denying food and drink to the poor at their Eucharistic assemblies, (1 Cor.11:22) and describes this unholy refusal as "contempt for the church of God". Jesus enabled people to have access to bread and to healing. Bread symbolizes all aspects of essential human need for sustenance and survival. To refuse to respond to the concrete brokenness of the human condition in favour of ritual observance is an obscenity.

The disciples on the road to Emmaus say to their unknown companion, "We were hoping that he was the one who would set Israel free." At a time when Palestine was being economically politically dominated by outside interests and economically exploited to serve those interests, they were not talking about spiritual liberation alone. This is the distortion that must be corrected.

CHAPTER FIVE

The Coming of Age of the Laity

Wisdom is not the quality of being wedded to the past.
Wisdom is the capacity to be devoted to its ideals.

Sister Joan Chittester, OSB

Jacques Maritain

The language used in this title is not new. The *coming of age of the laity* was an ongoing theme in the writings of Jacques Maritain, a Parisian lay Catholic and Thomist philosopher who represented in his moral sensitivities the Social Catholicism that arose from lay social involvement in France in the early part of the twentieth century. A child of the nineteenth century, Jacques Maritain came from a bourgeois, resolutely anticlerical and republican Parisian family. A convert to Catholicism in the first decade of the twentieth century, Maritain spent his life defending the Church's teaching in anticlerical France, always as a philosopher and never as a theologian. He envisioned an informed and empowered laity as the remedy for the Church's indifference to social conditions and subsequent declining ability to reach the unbelieving French proletariat. Unlike many who seek out the Church for more ignoble reasons, Maritain became a Catholic in a cultural Parisian world that disdained the institution, and viewed religious faith as a form of self-imposed and perpetual psychological adolescence.

His writings, academic and popular, reveal how much he loved the Church. He was clear-eyed about its strengths and its weaknesses, especially the detrimental effects of a communally introverted clericalism. When he visited Quebec in the 1940's, he told a friend that "the Church in Quebec was about blow". A decade or so later, his perceptive diagnosis was realized at an unprecedented level as the French Canadian clergy persisted in their blind resistance to change, a form of self-destructiveness that resembled that of their European cousins a century before. Recently in an article in a University of Milan publication, *Vita et Pensiero*, Cardinal Marc Ouellet of Quebec City, a church leader who also carried the title of Primate of Canada, described his province as a missionary territory, where less than one per cent of baptized Catholics were active in their parishes, and only five per cent attended Mass. (Globe and Mail, October 23rd, 2008) In France, even before the Second World War, this had become a standard diagnosis of French society by Catholic theologians. In Paris today, three per cent of families baptize their children. Clerical intransigence has its price.

Raised in an intellectually cultivated *haute bourgeois* family in Paris, Jacques Maritain studied at the Lycée Henri IV and at the Sorbonne, where he met Raissa Oumansoff, the daughter of Russian Jewish immigrants. At first attracted to Spinoza, he was introduced to the philosophy of Henri Bergson who was then teaching at the secular *Collège de France* by the Catholic socialist writer, poet and polemicist Charles Péguy. Both he and Raissa were disillusioned by the spiritual aridity of French positivism, and began seeking other alternatives for their lives, including the possibility of joint suicide. Maritain encountered the theology of Thomas Aquinas through the social Catholic writer Léon Bloy, and in 1906, the latter presided over their baptisms into the Catholic Church. After completing post-graduate studies at Heidelberg, Maritain taught philosophy in Paris, at first at the Lycée Stanislas, and later at the Institut Catholique.

In one of the first gestures of his election to the papacy in 1878, Leo XIII recognized St. Thomas Aquinas' theology as pre-eminent in the Church. Maritain's commitment to the Church was unqualified and determined, but also informed by the anticlericalism and unbelief that had become normative in French cultural life, not only among academically trained, critical intellectuals but throughout the middle and working classes. He and Raissa held weekly discussion groups in their apartment in an effort to make theological ideas, biblical studies and political discussion available to lay Catholics who were eager to inform the values of French society with their Christian commitment to the Gospel.

In the nineteen forties, vehemently opposed to the Vichy regime in France, he came to North America where he was greatly influenced by American democratic institutions and culture, especially the Catholic labour organizations that fought for a just wage. Unlike France, America was defined by the separation of Church and State and yet there was little evidence in the Catholic American experience of the bitter opposition in his French homeland. This five-year period of exile would transform his French Catholic defensiveness against the Bill of Rights defined by the Revolution and its anticlerical aftermath, toward a new appreciation of the importance of the American emphasis on human rights, and of the historical evangelical inspiration behind the development of democratic government. He came to this understanding late in his life. Another French social Catholic, the lay social activist Marc Sangnier had advanced this argument in the first decade of the twentieth century and was ecclesiastically condemned for it. Maritain would later be invited to participate in the UNESCO discussions leading up to the Declaration on Human Rights by the United Nations in 1948. This experience enabled him during Vatican Two to influence Paul VI personally and to support John Courtney Murray S.J. through persuasive debate on the floor in his effort to influence the bishops in attendance to change the Church's position on freedom of religious conscience. The emphasis on the right of truth as an abstraction was transformed into an emphasis on the right of the individual to discover the truth, without duress or imposition.

Maritain was also invited to teach at St. Michael's Institute of Medieval Studies in Toronto, where his ideas about an integral humanism and the primacy of the spiritual, his enthusiam for American democracy, as well as his alignment with the values of French social Catholicism informed the curriculum for later generations. His political concerns seem dated today. He took strong public positions against the rise of fascism and Nazism during the thirties, and was always arguing for the freedoms of religious institutions against the suppression of these rights by the anticlerical republican French state. Maritain accepted until his death the elevated position of monastic spirituality in the Church, and in middle age, he and Raissa took vows to cease their marital relations. After her death, he joined a monastic community, *Les Petits Frères de Jésus* in Toulouse where he remained until his death in 1973. Nonetheless, throughout his life he argued for a worldly holiness.

The meaning of the Second Vatican Council is only comprehensible against the history of previous centuries, especially the response of the Council at Trent in Italy to the Protestant Reformation and a similar reaction of the church at Vatican One to the Enlightenment, when the doctrine of papal infallibility was decided and proclaimed. From the time of the Reformation, and more especially after the French Revolution, the Vatican maintained a determined intellectual immunity to the critique of Christian Reform and later of modernity. The Protestant emphasis on freedom of conscience and the centrality of the Bible during the Renaissance was succeeded by the intellectual reaction of the enlightenment philosophers to the religious wars that ensued. Among these intellectual critics, the God of the Deists, a remote, disengaged presence apprehended by reason replaced in the popular mind the God of the Judaeo-Christian tradition, a God who is engaged with the world and its inhabitants through personal revelation, guided by the biblical spiritual and moral tradition, and apprehended by religious faith in addition to natural reason. Throughout Europe during these five centuries, the power of authoritarian monarchs was gradually mitigated by the rise of legislative assemblies, at first the nobility, then the landed gentry, and with the chaotic onset of the French Revolution, eventually the participation of the unschooled masses.

Throughout the nineteenth century, the institutional Catholic Church resisted these new cultural and political developments, and it is this more immediate history that Vatican Two was intended to address. Gregory

XVI (1831-1846) and Pius IX (1846-1878) officially condemned the new emphasis on human rights and on the democratization of state power, and opposed the new secularism, liberalism, and rationalism –modernity in all its aspects, as they yearned for the restoration of the *ancien regime* and the ecclesial privileges and security of place that this traditional political apparatus offered to the institutional church. Throughout the western world, even in South America, democracy and secularism brought new demands for separation of Church and State, i.e. the end of mandatory tithes and other privileges for the clergy, the laicization of education, the loss of church property, the repression of the monasteries, and the expulsion of religious orders. Bishops who resisted were banished or imprisoned. Pius IX spent the thirty-two years of his papacy defending papal power, authority, property and imperial privilege. When elected, he was considered a progressive in political matters, certainly more open-minded than his predecessor, but after the various European revolutions of 1848 and the turmoil that followed, including persistent demands for the democratization of the Church, Pius IX was forced to flee the Quirinale in disguise, as Garibaldi and Victor Emmanuel claimed the building as the seat of the newly unified Italian government. After this, he no longer favoured any kind of democratic reform.

Pius IX published 38 encyclicals including the dogma of the Immaculate Conception of Mary, (1854), encouraging devotion to the Sacred Heart throughout the entire Catholic world (1856), and the promulgation of papal infallibility (1870) at Vatican I. What defined his papacy, however, was the encyclical Quanta Cura, condemning the errors of the age, sixteen propositions in all, accompanied by the Syllabus of Errors, (1864), eighty more propositions which included the condemnation of pantheism, naturalism, rationalism, indifferentism, socialism, communism, freemasonry and the various kinds of religious liberalism then prominent as a response to the enlightenment critique of Christianity. This established within the institutional culture a pattern of reaction rather than engagement that continues to this day in many dioceses.

On the political level, the popular movement for the unification of Italy took on new life in 1859, as Victor Emmanuel II of Piedmont secured the grand duchy of Tuscany, and the duchies of Modena, Parma and Romagna.

In the following year, with the assistance of Giuseppe Garibaldi, King Victor Emmanuel II brought Sicily into the union and successfully united the southern region as far north as Naples, including the Papal States. In 1870, the Italian army entered the duchy of Rome, and took over the papal palace, the Quirinale, as the seat of the Italian government. Rome became the capital of Italy, and in 1871, the pope was granted the rights of a sovereign, and given an annual remuneration, but never again would the papacy be a temporal power with a standing army of its own. Pius IX and subsequent popes considered themselves prisoners of the Vatican until the three Lateran Treaties were negotiated with Benito Mussolini in 1929, creating the city state of Vatican City.

The papacy of Leo XIII would be remembered differently than that of his predecessor. The rise of republican democratic governments throughout Europe after the Franco-Prussian War in 1870 would bring new issues to the attention of Catholic lay elites concerned with the exploitation of the worker, as the industrial revolution and the widespread development of factories took hold. At first these efforts were the benevolent acts of the wealthy and influential to reduce the social alienation and personal degradation of young men flooding into urban centres from the country. But as labour unions formed, often under communist or socialist leadership, the issues of a living wage, safe working conditions, child labour, the length of the work day and week, decent housing, and popular education came to be seen as practical concerns for Catholics. These were the beginnings of social Catholicism. Sympathetic priests and lay leaders sought to support these workers, training them for leadership in their unions, and encouraging the development of local cooperatives to alleviate their struggle to provide for their families. From these bodies would issue the contents of Leo XIII 's encyclical Rerum Novarum, the encyclical that awakened the international Catholic conscience to social responsibility. An aristocrat and gifted intellectual, Leo XIII intended to reconcile the church with secularism, science with religion, and reason with faith.

His successor, Pius X, from humble circumstances, did not continue these directions with the same understanding or commitment. His interests favoured pious practices like the frequent reception of the Eucharist and internal concerns such as the reform of canon law. However, with the passing of time, his papacy is remembered for his condemnation of modernist theologians and ideas within the Church, and for his ambivalent commitment to lay bodies engaged in promoting the new social ethics, especially when these were accompanied by a critical lay spirit toward the Church itself. The Catholic laymen in Italy who sought to participate in politics were threatened with excommunication because the unification of Italy had led to the loss of church property, and the increasingly popular republican ideas were hostile to Church privilege and to a perceived religious indifference to the material wellbeing of the working poor. Anticlericalism had become rampant throughout Europe, not just among the educated elites but especially throughout the working classes.

Pius X and successive popes were sensitive to the absence of the working class in European parishes and were supportive of lay apostolates as long as they were serving only a cultural agenda, the apostolic interests of the Church. Political engagement was beyond this purview. At the local level, the ideals of social Catholicism continued to be promoted, especially through youth groups, agricultural and industrial workers, and civic employees. The first official Roman acknowledgements of the role of the laity occurred during the first decade of the twentieth century. These lay Catholic movements remained numerous if marginalized in Germany, Italy, France, Belgium, French Canada and elsewhere until Vatican Two, when the role of the Church in the modern world, and a new appreciation of the democratic responsibilities of the laity in the church as well as in society would change the Church forever. This shifting paradigm of lay participation came from German, French, Austrian, Swiss and Belgian theologians who would argue for a different kind of Church. These ideas are still being debated, and in some cases, thwarted, because of the challenge they represent to institutional cultures unwilling to change.

Yves Congar, O.P.

The expression, *the coming of age of the laity,* appears regularly in the writings of the Dominican theologian, Yves Congar. Congar was perhaps the most comprehensive and influential intellectual voice in the deliberations of the bishops at Vatican Two. When Congar died at the age of

91 on June 22^{nd,} 1995 at Les Invalides in Paris, he was hailed a few days later in a headline in the New York Times as a "vigorous ecumenist and promoter of the laity". He had been made a cardinal of the Church the year before. The French state had previously awarded him the Croix de Guerre, made him a Knight of the Légion d'Honneur, and a member of the Académie Française. During a period of fertile theological production in the Catholic Church, he stands among the most eminent and influential, and as a priest, he is remembered as a man who sought the truth over personal ambition, and the health and wellbeing of the Church over power and personal comfort.

The challenges he identified and struggled to realize made greater demands on Catholic clergy and bishops, as he sought the formation of priests who were not passive acolytes, but *prophetic forces* in their communities. He was preoccupied with the reasons for unbelief, and was not afraid to identify the deficiencies of the Church itself as contributing factors. He sought above all a church of adult lay Catholics, apostolic and influential in society but also in the church. Only emotionally and spiritually mature priests and bishops can endure the presence of emotionally and spiritually mature lay people, and this above all was his goal. Just as he expected Catholics to step outside their denominational comfort zone and enter into meaningful dialogue with Protestant Christians, he also expected the laity to provide a moral and spiritual leadership to the secular societies in which they lived and worked. While he recognized that spiritual poverty in the service of God required a faithful submission to the promptings of the Holy Spirit, he valued the modern emphasis on human freedom as the central core and dignity of the human person, as the place where the Spirit forms the conscience and feeds the soul.

Yves Marie-Joseph Congar was born in 1904 and grew up in Sedan in the Ardennes, not far from the Belgian border. During the First World War, Sedan was again occupied by the Germans, and the Catholic parish church the family attended was destroyed. Throughout the war, Catholics celebrated Sunday Mass in the local Protestant church. His best friends included both a Protestant and a Jewish boy from the neighbourhood. He entered the Carmelites in his twenties, and studied at the Institut Catholique. There he was introduced to Jacques Maritain by the Thomist professor, Daniel Lallement, but after three years, in 1925, Congar joined the Dominicans at Amiens, taking the name, Marie-Joseph. He completed his seminary studies at Le Saulchoir, then near Tournai in Belgium, and was ordained in 1930. There he met Marie-Dominique Chenu and Ambroise Gardeil who introduced him to the philosophical ideas of Maurice Blondel, especially *Le Donné révélé et la théologie*. Chenu awakened in him a new appreciation of the significance of the historical dimension of reality, and he admitted in an interview in 1975 that Congar and he had rediscovered Johann Adam Mohler, (1796-1838), a German historian and Catholic theologian associated with the Tubingen School, especially his conception of faith which integrated its historical, psychological and pastoral dimensions. Congar would affirm that Mohler had been an *éveilleur*, an animator of his thought for forty years. Mohler moved from a pneumatological approach to the Church emphasizing the Holy Spirit to a Christological one. Congar adopted the pneumatological approach, an emphasis on the freedom of the activity of the Holy Spirit in the Church that he would write about again and again until his death in 1995.

From 1925 until 1939, Congar was active in *Action Catholique*, an apostolic lay association in France and Belgium committed to social reform with the encouragement of Pius XI. He was part of a movement of priests and laity that acknowledged the loss of a sense of God's presence and activity in human consciousness that was the result of the Enlightenment's confidence in reason. Religious faith was replaced by a commitment to humanist ideals, the humanitarian ideals of justice and tolerance. They accepted however, the Enlightenment critique of power and authority and its impetus toward democratic, republican government. This experience of dedicated lay Catholics would become a formative influence in his advocacy of a theology specific to the laity as he began to appreciate that a new ecclesiology was necessary to address the atheistic secularism and widespread unbelief in his once very Catholic country. It would be the laity and not the clergy for the most part who would socially interact with this secularized population. Congar believed that the laity could also assist in freeing the Church from its defensive and isolationist tendencies.

During the thirties, Yves Congar was the first Catholic theologian to become actively engaged in the ecumenical movement, then a Protestant phenomenon, and in 1936, he gave a series of lectures in Paris on this theme. During a retreat in 1929 prior to ordination, in a meditation on the Trinitarian reality in John's gospel, "That they may be one as we are one", he believed he was being called by God to address Christian denominationalism and sectarianism, deeming a divided Christendom to be a countersign to the nature of the Trinity and opposed to the will of God. With the support of his community, he visited the major sites associated with Martin Luther, and studied the Protestant theologians, especially Karl Barth and Oscar Cullman by attending courses in the Protestant Faculty of Theology in Paris. In 1937, Congar published *Chrétiens Déunis: principes d'un Oecumenisme catholique,* the first volume on ecumenism in French and also the first of the Unam Sanctam series, published by Éditions du Cerf. Congar accepted the charge of conservatives that Vatican Two had contributed to the protestantization of the Catholic Church in its adoption of the vernacular in the liturgy, emphasis on the study of scripture, the increased initiative of local churches to respond to their own particular pastoral needs, and the acceptance of a variety of lay charisms which sometimes diminishes the position of the formally ordained. He sustained this commitment, writing, preaching, and teaching about ecumenism until his death.

Congar was part of a movement with the European Catholic community between 1930 and 1960 to respond to the atheistic secularism that had become the dominant culture of the European intelligentsia. He became one of the chief architects of a new ecclesiology that embraced the laity as active subjects in the Church. In his thorough and comprehensive grasp of Congar's writings, the Irish priest and academic, Gabriel Flynn, has identified Yves Congar's gradually developing conviction that unbelief in France was the single most important factor driving his research, an unbelief directly related to the deficiencies of the Church, a position shared by the Jesuit theologians, Jean Daniélou and Henri de Lubac.[1] In 1935, after three years of investigation, he published an article entitled *Conclusion théologique à l'enquête sur les raisons actuelles de l'incroyance,* in a French Catholic journal, *la Vie intellectuelle,* where he lays out his conclusions about the causes of unbelief for so many of his countrymen, an unbelief being perpetuated from one generation to another. His theological interests were always pastoral. He rejected a theological enterprise turned in upon itself. He believed that a juridico-hierarchical model of the church created the effect of a harsh and condemning judge, and led to a poor presentation of the humanity and mercy of Christ and of his grace in the world.

With the rejection of democratic republicanism by the Church until the papacy of Leo XIII, the upper, educated, political classes of France had become more and more anti-clerical, and this animosity gradually led to the dechristianization of French society. From secular critics and politicians of the nineteenth and twentieth centuries, there is a long list of accusations: oppressive authoritarianism and disregard for human rights, opposition to the exercise of freedom of conscience, a negative appreciation of the quality of psychological, emotional and sexual life, a preoccupation with the control of information and a rejection of new ideas that advanced the intellectual liberation of individuals, and a disregard for a fundamental humanism. For the workers of the lower classes, the issues were related more to their material needs. Living conditions in the slums were unhygienic, violent, appalling, and the only remedy the parish Church provided was a faithful ritual observance and prayer, an ecclesiological conviction proceeding from the seventeenth century. This would lead Congar eventually to a preoccupation with church reform. Congar was determined to replace the juridico-hierarchical image that the Church had presented to the world since Gregory VII's struggle with the temporal European powers in the eleventh century, an image that had been reiterated at the Council of Trent, with biblical images that reflected the mystery of Christ's loving presence - the people of God, the light of the world, as well as more recent church images, the Body of Christ, the Temple of the Holy Spirit etc. He also sought to rearticulate ideas about God and faith, revelation and grace.

Until the war, Congar taught theology at Le Saulchoir, the Dominican seminary where he was now working alongside Marie-Dominique Chenu and Henri-Marie Féret. He gradually came to understand through new eyes the Modernist controversy and the papal censure that had halted and stymied the efforts of Catholic theologians to address modernity early in the century. Modernism was the name given to the introduction into the Church of the historical critical method in biblical historical studies and interpretation, drawing on the new critical social sciences including anthropology, which was still in its infancy, historiography, and literary analysis. Originating from German Protestantism, this new interest in the Bible led to an innovative and fertile theological period in the Church, also in the world religions and concerning the psychological nature of revelation. It must be said that sometimes flawed attempts were made to reconcile the Church to modernity. Condemned by Pius X in 1907, dissenting theologians were excommunicated and careers ruined, as the Vatican overreacted in an absolutist and repressive way. Congar judged the condemnation to be shallow and "purely negative", coming from a theological community removed from the needs and questions of the people the Church exists to serve. Cardinal Angelo Roncalli, following his role in Paris as Apostolic Nuncio, understood this dynamic and Vatican Two was called to address questions dating from the Modernist period, and to restore the Church's relationship with the modern world.

With Jean Daniélou, M.-D. Chenu, Henri de Lubac, Karl Rahner, and Joseph Ratzinger, Congar spearheaded the method of *ressourcement*, returning to biblical, patristic, and liturgical sources in order to present a more animated faith to his contemporaries struggling with belief and unbelief. Together they embarked on an enterprise to eliminate what they called "the baroque theology of the Counter-Reformation", by creating a new theological series, Unam Sanctam. Congar encouraged the Jesuit, Henri de Lubac, the product of an active social Catholic family, to write *Catholicisme: les aspects sociaux de dogme (1938)* addressing the problem of an extremely individualized and privatized religious sensibility among Catholics. Congar was a pre-eminent practitioner of this method. Curiously, decades before, the poet and social critic Charles Péguy had also recommended a return to the sources. Following the Second War, *ressourcement* helped to liberate Protestantism from a naïve liberalism and an oppressive fundamentalism, traps that Karl Barth urged Catholic theologians not to fall into. Barth also showed Catholics how it is possible to read the Gospel in ways that are faithful both to historical faith and to the methods of historical criticism. In Catholicism, *ressourcement* helped to liberate Catholic theologians from the oppressive irrelevance of neo-scholastic classical idealism, the mainstream theology that had become divorced from history, spirituality and pastoral concerns. The influential Réginald Garrigou-Lagrange would dub this new approach, *la nouvelle théologie* and he severely criticized the developing movement. By 1947, Pius XII was expressing his concerns to the superiors of the Dominican and Jesuit communities.

Congar was drafted into the French army as a chaplain, and spent the years from 1940 to 1945 as a prisoner of war in the prisons of Colditz and Lübeck in Germany. The impact of a different kind of comradeship during the war, even in the prison camps, cannot be overestimated as an influence on his thinking, as he came to see that the rejection of the Church by so many was more complex than he had understood. The issue of unbelief in the modern world became central to his understanding of the task of the Church. After the war, he returned to teach at Le Saulchoir, and became an advocate and defender of the worker-priest movement in France, as many French clergy sought to identify their lives with the conditions and concerns of the urban working classes. Unlike North America, the Church in France had been marked for centuries by a noteworthy identification with the social influence of the aristocracy and the wealth and power of the *haute bourgeoisie*. The higher clergy hailed from the upper and educated classes, and were disengaged from the struggles to better the conditions of the working class. The Vatican shut down the movement in 1953, when Angelo Roncalli was the Apostolic Nuncio in Paris. Perhaps because of the controversy this provoked throughout France, there is no doubt that John XXIII came to appreciate the need to create a parish culture where an adult laity could function with agency and meaningful participation. When he wrote to the bishops all over the world a month before Vatican Two began in 1962, he asked them to reflect on how the Church might address the needs of all, but especially the needs of the poor.

In 1951, the publication of the encyclical Humani generis by Pius XII had fallen into the old defensive pattern of papal condemnation of all things scientific and contemporary, evolution, existentialism etc. In 1950, Congar published *Vraie et Fausse Réforme dans l'Église* and in 1953, *Jalons pour une théologie du laïcat*, seeking to make the Church more pastoral. As was the case with Modernism, and is today with Liberation Theology, interest in *la nouvelle théologie* and the reaction it provoked spread far beyond church circles. Congar articulated the need for a "total ecclesiology" that would support a theology of the laity and foster a more active lay participation. Yves Congar understood, as did Fyodor Dostoyevski, the reluctance of many adults to respect and exercise their freedom, how easy it is to hide behind authority, to retreat behind convention or convenience when only conscience is pre-eminent, and moral choices must be made or publicly declared. It is difficult for us in the twenty-first century to recognize what a hot button issue freedom of conscience was for officialdom at this time.

In February 1954, Chenu, Féret, Congar and Pierre Boisselot were summoned to Paris by the master of the Dominican Order, and dismissed from their teaching posts at le Saulchoir. Congar chose to go to Jerusalem, and then to Blackfriars at Cambridge, finally returning to France in December, 1955 at the invitation of Mgr. Jean Weber, the bishop of Strasbourg, where the Dominicans have a centre dating back to medieval times. The University of Strasbourg continues to be one of the foremost European centres for ecumenical research and dialogue. In the old city, a Lutheran parish stands adjacent to a Catholic parish on the same property, both called St. Peters, their architecture identical and their buildings complementary. His ideas and reputation lay in the shadows, until he was called to Rome by John XXIII to consult on the documents being prepared for Vatican Two.

In an edited version of his conciliar diary, *Mon Journal du Concile*, published in 2002, seven years after his death, Congar described the hopelessness of that time, his disillusionment and discouragement over these documents as the Curia controlled the process.[2] Not until the end of the first session in December, 1962, when the bishops at the Council rejected the documents as pastorally deficient and unhelpful, did his hope for internal change recur. Over the next three years, he participated actively on a number of draft committees, using the depth of learning he had acquired in patristic and medieval theology, and in biblical and liturgical studies, to establish his credibility and trustworthiness. He contributed to the documents on missions, the clergy, ecumenism, religious freedom, the Church, the world religions, and the Church in the Modern World, which issued from commissions on both theology and the laity. He proved to be a man of patience and political realism, seeking realizable goals. But perhaps the most effective contribution he made during this time were the lectures he gave to informal gatherings of bishops in the evenings, where various progressive theologians would be invited to share and debate their views.

He addressed the absence of free opinion in the Church as detrimental to the internal life of the Church to the extreme, silencing not only the clergy but also the laity. He identified juridicism or legalism as the enemies of a culture where freedom of speech as an expression of adult behaviour is normative. The *lex privata Spiritus Sancti*, the relations of a person's conscience with God precede the church's canonical obligations. And so in the Constitution on the Church (iv, 37) we find: *An individual layman, (sic) by reason of the knowledge, competence, or outstanding ability which he (sic) may enjoy, is permitted and sometimes even obligated to express his (sic) opinion on things which concern the good of the Church.* This text does not advocate a thoughtless anarchy, an emotional rebelliousness, or an irresponsible capriciousness, but is attempting to protect the quest for freedom of spirit that characterizes adult conduct along with the Christian understanding of freedom to be the willingness to be a servant of God's will.

Yves Congar sought to present the divine mystery as a God of Life, as a liberating God, and the church as a sacrament of God's presence in the world, rooted in Scripture, bearing witness to Kingdom values and profoundly concerned for humankind. He would repeatedly use the expression, "a Church less of the world and more for the world," recognizing that a declericalization was necessary, a collective conversion to the lifestyle and values of Jesus, to a holy priesthood less interested in power and personal authority, and committed to service. He rejected any concept of the Church or of religion unconcerned for the world and its collective salvation. The church existed to serve the world, not to rule over it. In *Lumen Gentium*, the constitution on the Church, he argued for the expression, *the People of God*, even *the messianic people of God*, to define a community of equality in the eyes of God, implying a dynamic apostolic mission to the world, with a religious and moral obligation to address the material needs of the poor.

Congar also challenged the presentation of religion primarily as worship and moral obligations, the heritage of the seventeenth century, as responsible for depriving Catholics of a Christianity of eschatological hope, hope for the future, hope for the material world, hope of a fulfilment of the world in Jesus Christ. Gradually, a feudal, clerical Church was being replaced by a more dynamic, democratic, challenging and prophetic model. Everyone in the Church, in the people of God, was being challenged to a more demanding practice, not only of spiritual poverty, but of fighting against those institutions that keep the poor in a position of subjection and psychological bondage. The friendship he developed with Paul VI brought not only personal recognition as he was invited to serve on a new international Theological Commission, but also contributed to the pope's desire to use the Church's international presence to address the economic emancipation of the developing world.

In Congar's model of ministry, the laity exercises a decisive role against unbelief and religious indifference and the baneful personal and social effects these have for individual fulfilment, for the family and for society as a whole. He refused to accept the French reality of an increasing diminishing, ghettoized Church or the status quo based on ritual observance, with little pastoral provision at the parish level to foster a personal and adult faith. His vision of a Church inclusive of the laity was intended to realize the full potential of the people of God. He understood the holiness of the Church to be the distinctive concern of the Holy Spirit.

Vatican Two could not arrive at a definition of the lay state in the Church, falling back on the historical division between the ordained priest's responsibility for the spiritual domain, the laity's for the temporal and secular sphere. He regretted that language like *people of God* and *a messianic people* did not appear in *Gaudium et Spes*, the document on the Church and the Modern World. Congar rejected the medieval identification of the Church with the priesthood and found in the biblical term, *koinonia*, the community that God creates through the grace of divine self-revelation, an equality of God's presence that is shared by everyone. This communal image and the recognition that the Holy Spirit addresses everyone in the Church, not only the clergy, was intended to modify hierarchical assumptions in favour of a horizontal image of a community graced by multiple and different charisms. A genuine *sensus fidei* requires mutual respect and cooperation between the hierarchy and faithful. If the leadership is unwilling to provide a context where all lay voices can be heard, especially dissenting voices and not merely those in agreement, then all talk of a valid *sensus fidei* is meaningless. The tension between the peripheral and the prophetic, and the maintaining centre will always exist, and from it will come life and authenticity. Trust is not based on people holding similar ideas, but on a developing conviction that all are concerned for the authenticity and wellbeing of the Church, not just the clergy.

When Karl Rahner wrote the essay *A Church of Sinners* in his later years, he argued that it is impossible for the Church to claim that it has nothing to do with the sins of its members, since the church does not exist without its members[3] When the *Lumen Gentium* is reduced to nothing more than liturgical aesthetics and a social support for the upwardly mobile and for middle class respectability, the leadership is complicit. To portray the Church as independent of its sinful members is to misrepresent its true nature. Congar decried "the ruinous separation of the sacred from the profane, and the order of creation from the order of redemption". If the Spirit reveals our sinful nature to us, so does the Spirit also foster in us our creative capacities. If the members of a congregation are indifferent to the evil and injustice in their neighbourhood or in the society they live in, surely the leadership of that parish is complicit. Perhaps the answer is simpler than we would like to accept. Matthew promises that those who advance the cause of justice in the light of the Trinitarian reign of God will be persecuted, but he insists that like the prophets before them, they will also be blessed, and that this persecution is an indication that the reign of God is theirs. (5:10)

The theology of the laity advanced by Yves Congar has now been surpassed and developed by other Catholic theologians. The Catholic feminist biblical historian Elizabeth Schussler Fiorenza has acknowledged publicly that had she not met her husband Francis at the University of Munster, (where both were students of Joseph Ratzinger who reportedly continues to read her work), and emigrated to the United States, her life would have been entirely different. As a woman she would never have been hired by a German Catholic seminary to teach, as she was by Notre

Dame in Indiana before moving on to Harvard. Her historical research into the early church, and the specialized feminist biblical exegesis she has pursued will be challenging the hierarchical principle for generations to come. Her emphasis on the inclusive, egalitarian, table fellowship of Jesus, and her historical examination of the elimination of any record of female leadership in the early Church, challenge not only the patriarchal assumptions of Catholic ecclesiology and its bias toward a celibate and clerical system, but the fundamental misogyny and self-interest that underlines it in all Christian religious traditions. She is responsible for a new kind of exegesis called *a hermeneutic of suspicion* that questions any biblical or dogmatic statement about women as representing the possibility of male patriarchal distortion.

Nor is she alone. Nowhere in the world has the institutional Catholic church been challenged by the laity with the grass roots effectiveness that it has achieved in the United States. Subsequent to Vatican Two, Catholic universities and colleges in North America opened their seminaries and theology departments to lay students, male and female, and now more than half of those attending these academic graduate programs are lay. Research in all fields of theology, biblical, moral, fundamental, Christological, sacramental, pastoral, is being produced by Catholic lay men and women teaching in these institutions and providing a new way of looking at these disciplines. This does not mean that these well-intentioned scholars may not become co-opted into the clerical, hierarchical, white male, careerist agenda. Hopefully, like Elizabeth Schussler Fiorenza, they will provide a prophetic critique of the church and its lay community, and will not retreat into safe preoccupations with career mobility and the social acceptance of their more cautious academic peers.

In the nineteen nineties, when the scandal of clerical paedophilia broke in the media throughout North America, new Catholic lay organizations like *The Voice of the Faithful* in the Boston area arose to ensure that the offenders would be brought to justice and the legal rights of the victims acknowledged. Efforts on the part of the hierarchy to cover up these offences without regard for their impact on the victims shocked many Catholics to organize in their defence. Before becoming pope, Joseph Ratzinger was revealed to have demanded all legal documentation be sent to Rome so that it could not be used in the ensuing court cases. Clergy, all celibate and childless, and socially enculturated to protect the Church at the expense of the victims, collaborated to hide the evidence. To pay the millions of dollars of damages in the Boston area alone, the solution was to close churches. No thoughtful Catholic anymore questions the presence of sin in the Church. Present efforts by the American bishops to focus on the issues of contraception and abortion, especially during election cycles, fool only the gullible and uninformed.

Many years before, in 1976, *Call to Action*, a national lay organization was convened by the American bishops. It is now entirely lay directed and claims a membership of about 25,000 Catholic men, women, young people, nuns and clergy, with local chapters all over the country. Their national conference each November involves three days of lectures, films, liturgy and paraliturgy presented by theologians and various activist leaders, all reflecting a Vatican Two image of the Church as the people of God, empowered, initiating, informed, committed to social justice, and despite their critical consciousness, loyal and faithful to the Church. When controversial decisions are taken to include bodies such a Gay and Lesbian Catholics and the Women's Ordination Movement, the membership declines but always rises again. A threat in 2007 by a bishop in Wyoming to excommunicate active members from his diocese was greeted with laughter at the subsequent national conference and dismissed as the action of a irresponsible autocrat who was socially isolated from the moral consciousness of his flock. Similar groups by other names exist in Germany, Austria, Holland, Belgium, France and Italy.

In Canada, during the nineteen seventies, progressive Catholic newspapers, usually biweeklies, appeared, reflecting a spirituality that embraced social issues. One, in Muenster, Saskatchewan, published by the Benedictine monks of St. Peter's Abbey, continues. The other, New Catholic Times of Toronto, with a declining readership and lack of financial support, folded in 2005. During the revelations of paedophilia in the early nineties, an organization sprang up in Toronto, called the Coalition of Concerned Canadian Catholics to bring lay people together to ensure that the institutional leadership was held to account. Banned from Church premises, it functioned effectively for a few years, but due to poor and inappropriate leadership, this group did not survive. Lay informants from the Canadian Conference of Bishops were sent to investigate at the annual conferences, and reported back that there was a lot of whining going on. Canadians lack the democratic faith in ordinary people common to American life, the grass roots claim to participation that seems to be in their very bones. The democratization of the Catholic Church will not come out of Canada.

What Jacques Maritain and Yves Congar did not anticipate was the obscuring of the modes of engagement that would result over time between clergy and laity, as both men accepted the distinctive roles of the clergy and the laity. Today, with many lay people trained in theology, more and more theologically trained laity seem to restrict their life commitment to the Church alone, despite the horizon of social responsibility that was a part of their formation, and they retreat into an intra-ecclesial apostolate - paraliturgical leadership roles, bible study groups, retreats, etc. and provide neither leadership nor witness to the world beyond the Church. They might as well belong to a monastic order.

1. Gabriel Flynn, *Yves Congar's Vision of the Church in a World of Unbelief*, Aldershot and Burlington:Ashgate Publishing, 2004.

2. Yves Marie-Joseph Congar, *Mon Journal de Concile*, Paris:Les Éditions du Cerf, 2002.

3. Karl Rahner, "*A Church of Sinners*", Theological Investigations VI (pp.253-269).

CHAPTER SIX

Mary of Nazareth

Just as modern historical biblical research into the context of Jesus' life has shifted our emphasis from the divine to the human elements of his experience and purpose, so too has the historical context of the life of Mary, his mother, been reassessed. Since the nineteen seventies, Catholic nuns and laywomen have qualified in all branches of theology and are continually engaged in historical, theological and biblical research and writing. Armed with an appreciation of feminist theory, these determined women are challenging the cultural norms of Catholic seminaries and colleges. Female scholars look to Mary as they look to Jesus, not to idealize her beyond any aspect of recognizable humanity but to understand the challenges of her life and how she negotiated them, so that ordinary Catholic women may find in her an example of Spirited life that is personally empowering, an example that assists them in the daily struggles of their lives for dignity and self-realization.

In the past, Mary was lauded by religious men and women for those qualities that affirmed their own social education in gender roles. This was the case with Thérèse of Lisieux in my Catholic school where, humility and hiddenness were favorite themes: Mary's hidden support of Jesus and her unwillingness to claim for herself some of the sun, now we might say infamy, that his preaching and actions brought upon his family. This was before secular feminist scholars began to analyze how superficial or idealized female images and oppressive role models could be used to suppress the emergence and development of women and little girls. To mention only the earliest and finest voices, Elisabeth Schussler Fiorenza and Rosemary Radford Reuther were the first Catholic scholars to examine the functional and psychological use of Mary in the Catholic theological tradition in the light of contemporary aspirations for female emancipation and flourishing.

Elisabeth Schussler Fiorenza specialized in biblical theology at the University of Munster in Germany. She married an American theologian, Francis Fiorenza, and moved to the United States. She has focused her penetrating academic lens on the role of women as it has been presented or omitted in the canonical scriptural texts. She has developed new forms of exegesis to determine the historical role that women played in the early Christian communities, and she emphasizes the egalitarian and inclusive ideals of those communities, especially how these values were gradually surrendered to obscurity as the leadership sought a political and social accommodation with the patriarchal cultural norms of the Graeco-Roman world. Rosemary Radford Reuther is an American historian who as early as the late sixties, was locating the developing women's movement for human rights within a larger framework of international struggles for civil and economic rights, and she remains one of the clearest minded critics of Catholic ecclesial history and spirituality. Both women as academics have been too *hot* for the cultures of restricted academic freedom in Catholic academic institutions and have been associated with secular colleges and universities for many years.

My personal favorite is Sr. Elizabeth Johnson C.S.J. from Fordham University in New York City who has written extensively in Christology and Mariology. Johnson has situated Mary in the political, social, economic and religious world of Galilee in the early part of the first century and presents her as an ally and sister of women seeking to find their own independent identity and voice in an otherwise civilized Western culture where male privilege and cultural power underpins every institutional culture. I am much indebted to her original insight and thorough understanding of the Marian tradition.[1]

In 1990, a Sri Lankan Oblate theologian, Fr. Tissa Balasuriya, in an essay that became a book, addressed the historical and political factors that led to the Church's obsession with the doctrine of original sin and he outlines the subsequent consequences of this dogma for many branches of theology – soteriology, Christology, Mariology etc.[2] Governed by a respect for historical data and the critical consciousness of a hermeneutic of suspicion, he has challenged the male presuppositions, assumptions and self-interest of theologians who consciously or not, seek to satisfy the needs of a group of believers who exercise dominant political, cultural and spiritual power in both ecclesial and secular society. As a man of the developing world, trained originally in political science before entering the priesthood, Fr. Balasuriya thinks in collective terms, not just in personal and private ones, and has spent his life as a priest concerned with the impact of poverty and illiteracy on the lives of his fellow citizens. He has replaced the traditional individualistic and other-worthy interpretations of Mary with a more concrete one that is historically informed and that acknowledges the communitarian dimension of salvation. What distinguishes all of these theologians is that they are writing for the entire Church, not just for the academic validation of the theological community, and so their work is accessible, startling, original and prophetic.

For me during the nineteen fifties, the Catholic parish was a place of personal liberation and empowerment, a community where my talents and qualities of leadership were discovered and affirmed. But I gained a new awareness of clerical patriarchal self-interest in my late twenties when I was asked by a former principal, a sister of St. Joseph, to pursue theological studies at the graduate level, and the two priests who had previously functioned as my spiritual advisors, one a Jesuit Dean of Studies in Toronto, the other a diocesan priest living at Madonna House in Combermere, attempted to discourage me from doing this. I had naively expected both of them to be thrilled by my decision.

Yet, the school of theology at St. Michael's College in Toronto was an encouraging environment for me. For the first time in my experience, priests rejoiced in my intelligence and did not attempt to discourage my pursuit of academic and personal excellence. I attribute this sense of acceptance to their celibate state as they did not view me as "date" material. Years later, when my review of an academic work by a European Lutheran biblical scholar in a local Catholic paper was published, I was confronted by two highly qualified liberationist priests in Toronto offended by my intrusion into *their* world and expertise. Intelligent, theologically trained Catholic women are fine as long as they remain silent and validate men it seems. Lay colleagues in Catholic education have been more oppressive and damaging to my reputation and career than the many well educated and socially committed priests that I have known. Most of the nuns that I worked with at that time were also not so generous, and I determined never again to work with religious women as my employer.

Like so many Catholic women of my generation, Mary, the mother of Jesus, was an important image of holy femininity from a young age. Barely seven and five, my sister and I built a small altar for her in our bedroom and picked fresh flowers from the garden when they were available. My mother was not pleased as we had used one of her better linen cloths. A long treasured white china statue of Mary still stands beside my bed, although her European likeness is a distortion of her true Palestinian darkness of hair and complexion. It is not however the statue of my young adulthood. In my thirties, I smashed that one to the floor, having come to an appreciation of the negative effects that particular religious devotion had exercised over my life. Mary was foremost of the saints for Catholic girls largely because of her identification with sexual virginity, the only kind of purity that mattered it seems. My imagination was particularly taken with the image, *star of the sea,* as she is presented in Leonard Cohen's hymn to womanhood, *Suzanne,* standing atop Notre Dame des Bonsecours in the old port of Montreal, guiding sailors safely home, a church beloved of my father. Protector and safeguard, eager servant of God, simple, uneducated woman of faith, these were not insignificant attributions.

But I had begun to seek other role models, usually women in secular political life who had emancipated themselves from the constrictions of past generations and were fighting for other emancipatory values for women, and against gender assumptions that warred against female flourishing.

I was particularly conscious in secondary school education of social and economic obstacles determining the lives of young women called *the feminization of poverty*. Young females from traditional working class cultures especially, when confronting learning difficulties and discouragement, would exchange school for early pregnancy due to a reductive social equation of female value to childbearing in the world they inhabited. No teacher is unaware of the impact of socio-economic factors on student achievement or that the lives of children are determined by the literacy levels as well as the educational expectations of their mothers and sometimes their fathers. It is a painful process fraught with a sense of disloyalty to challenge the values of one's mother's life.

In Catholic spirituality, Mary has been used to replicate the patriarchal understanding of male/female relations: the young woman submissive to the will of God to promote female subordination to men as the feminine ideal. The elevation of virginal purity in Catholic cultures has succeeded in creating hierarchies of holiness among women within the church itself by suggesting different levels of spiritual quality between nuns and their lay sisters, instead of promoting communities of religious solidarity and mutual support among these women. Hispanic American psychologists use the term *marianismo* to describe a socially learned set of behaviours to address problems of self-esteem and conflicted gender identity in their clients. In a study called *The Maria Paradox*, marianismo identifies and advances a feminine spiritual superiority through a life of self-sacrifice in order to please men and to serve the interests of the family.[3] In cultures where devotion to Mary is still strong, Catholic women still struggle more than most to claim a right to significant involvement in public and political life. Here too the mother is important. Similarly, institutional churches that promote most actively Marian devotion and piety are least likely to welcome the participation and leadership of women. Relegated to service of the family or of the Church, their larger dreams and aspirations are discouraged or more frequently ignored or not acknowledged. This restrictive ideal of human fulfilment and its subsequent constriction of female social roles interrupt and thwart the development of female autonomy and moral growth, but also an independent autonomy, the acquiring of an identity independent of father or husband, the realization of one's talents and abilities through educational and career achievement, even social or political leadership.

As the negative use of the Marian symbol has been exposed by professionally trained Catholic women, devout Catholic women have begun to move beyond this deforming, repressive cult of an often manipulative and certainly infantilizing female passivity and docility by identifying their own self-defeating behaviours. Primary is a learned helplessness or a willing acceptance of the back burner usually as the encouraging cheerleader for the men in their lives. Sometimes this amounts to a patient submissiveness in the face of physical or verbal abuse by fathers, brothers or lovers, intended usually to preserve marital and domestic peace, all without the support of the androcentric culture of their Church which continues to exploit their service but to marginalize their leadership and to maintain a culpable silence about their hidden and often shamefully silent oppression.

Catholic female scholars have come to appreciate how Mary has been used for millennia to service patriarchal psychology and male privilege in the Church and in the family. The clergy may prefer a woman who willingly and selflessly serves the Church through her contribution to parish life or religious education or Catholic school leadership to another who presents herself as a theological scholar and critical voice, just as many Catholic men prefer domesticated wives who serve their families and attend their husband's arrival at the end of the day to women engaged in their own professional responsibilities or political interests. In contrast to the privileges and titles attributed to Mary through male dominated dogmatic pronouncement, interest in Mary as a historical participant in the mission of Jesus has accompanied the explosion of new knowledge now available about the time and culture of Jesus through recent anthropological, archaeological and sociological investigation. Mary's pilgrimage of faith occurred at a time when only wealthy women exercised any public or social influence. In contrast, Mary came from a poor rural peasant village culture, was probably illiterate, certainly politically powerless, and so feminist scholars attempt to rediscover aspects of her real lived experience so that she will not continue to be misused by those who oppose contemporary emancipatory female dreams. As Sr. Elizabeth Johnson has claimed, they seek to present Mary as a companion, as a sister in their own struggle for voice and for fullness of life.

As women have come to understand the myriad ways that female behaviour has been contained by male power and social influence, they have begun to emerge from the psychological imprisonment of the sexist imagination through a mutual and shared emancipatory struggle. Many have come to recognize that the Church, instead of representing the liberating empowerment of divine justice through its teaching and practice, has contributed to society's ease in devaluing women's unique qualities, often focusing on female sexual power and influence, exploiting female generosity and willingness to serve, but remaining publicly silent and indifferent to female struggles for dignity and self-respect. For many Catholic women unaware of this new theological understanding, a negative symbolism of Mary in the midst of a worldwide movement for female emancipation has made of her a despised if not irrelevant religious symbol.

Mary came from an uneducated backwater culture and would have been subject to the physical and psychological expressions of male silencing, domination, dismissal, aggression and violence commonplace in patriarchal cultures and still deeply entrenched in traditional patriarchal family, institutional and social relationships today. Female theologians have sought to recover this historical Mary, the woman who at first objected to and then struggled to support her son in his dangerous prophetic vocation, whose social powerlessness left her faithful but impotent as she witnessed his public humiliation and death, and who became a disciple and provided stalwart support of his young and tenuous community after his death. This young woman makes her own difficult decisions with courage and determination, and questions God's intentions with the angel for herself and for the life of her son. After finding him discussing theology in the Temple with the Jewish elders, *she ponders these things in her heart*. When he leaves the rejection of Nazareth for Capernaum to begin his public ministry, she is concerned and worried about the prophetic road he has taken and tries to prevent it. Nonetheless, she is present at the end of his life in Jerusalem, in the midst of helpless confusion and public humiliation, and later in the post-Resurrection scene of the upper room, she awaits with male and female disciples, the outpouring of the Spirit.

As I have come to appreciate the prophetic nature of Jesus' mission, I have also begun to view Mary differently. She would have been his first religious teacher and guide. The man he became must have issued from her influence on him as a child and young man. Never was I informed of the implications of the story in the gospel of Mark 3:31-35 where his mother *and brothers and sisters* come to take him home from a place where he is preaching. She was clearly shown in that account *not* to be a part of his community of disciples and was opposed to the direction he had taken. This is the story of Mary that Protestants are raised with. Better than most, Mary must have understood the challenge Jesus was presenting to the political and religious status quo, and the danger this represented not just to Jesus but also to the members of his family in that politically torn Roman colony. This also suggests that the prophetic Jewish values that he was preaching had implications for the Roman invaders, and not just for elite Jewish religious interests who would have understood them more clearly.

Matthew places Mary in a genealogical line of controversial women when he relates the story of the virgin birth and places Mary with other women at the foot of the cross. Luke presents her with more complexity as a young woman of stalwart faith and a woman identified with the poor and powerless in the Magnificat. Nonetheless, Luke presents a series of women, from Anna the prophetess and wife of Simeon to Mary of Bethany, the sister of Lazarus who listen but do not speak. The Greek word, diakonia or service, a word used to describe various ministries in the early Church, is used to describe the work Martha was doing and it was not housework. In John's gospel, it is Martha and not Peter who proclaims that that Jesus is "the Christ, the Son of God, the one who is coming into the world", suggesting that she was a leader in the early Christian community. (John 11:27) This is a gender paradigm that Luke continues through the Acts of the Apostles.

According to Paul, women were active in many ministries in these communities; often they were wealthy women with social influence who provided their properties for gatherings and worship. A patriarchal Jewish man, Paul often recognizes the dedicated leadership and determination of these women. Yet the example Jesus provided in his egalitarian relations with women seems already to have become obscured. John identifies

Mary's influence with Jesus in the story of the marriage at Cana, and places her at the cross and in the upper room in Jerusalem among other male and female disciples awaiting the outpouring of the Spirit. She is never mentioned during the heart of Jesus' ministry and her absence in the gospels suggests that she becomes a disciple only at the end of his life. This is all the gospels tell us about her. Everything else that is claimed about Mary is part of the tradition of the Church but has no canonical scriptural foundation. From later apocryphal writings and extra-canonical sources such as the Protoevangelium of James, we learn the identity of her parents Joachim and Anna, who were aged and childless before she was born and of her dedication in the Temple at the age of three, how Anna proclaimed, *My soul doth magnify the Lord*, how Mary and Joseph had seven sons etc. How much of this represents historical accuracy, how much Jewish midrash, symbolic interpretation more interested in conveying meaning rather than historical accuracy, is unclear.

Despite the many official privileges and titles bestowed on Mary – Mother of God, Queen of Heaven, Mother of the Church etc., the idealization of the feminine that she represents in Catholic theology has not been emancipatory for women, although a sexually segregated religious life and the necessity of running educational and medical institutions often provided such opportunity for female religious living in community. Excessive glorification of Mary as immaculately conceived or as virgin mother was used as a religious and social denigration of the many. Many educated, thoughtful women have abandoned the Church because of its historical contribution to sexist ideology and female oppression in the patriarchal family. To remedy this misuse of Mary, feminist biblical scholars adopt a hermeneutic of suspicion in their investigation of the biblical, extra-canonical and oral tradition about her. Who is making this claim about Mary and why is he making this claim?

Sr. Elizabeth Johnson presents Mary as a friend of God and of prophets within the circle of all those who seek God, the company of saints, living and dead. Ivone Gebara and Maria Clara Bingemen from Brazil approach Mary from the perspective of the Latin American world as poor women are beginning to claim their voice in a broader struggle of the poor for decent living conditions, educational opportunity, employment etc.[4] A philosopher by training, Gebara addresses the subtle underpinnings of dualistic Platonic idealism on Catholic spirituality that distract our attention and appreciation from the reality of the world we live in with all its beauty and repulsiveness, joy and heartbreak. These theologians seek a more human-centred anthropology, where men and women together participate as equals in the shaping of history. This theological method "from below", from the ground of history rather than from the heights of Greek abstraction of what could or should be, has altered our understanding of the reign or kingdom of God. As Gustavo Gutierrez has pointed out, we must pass through not only the dark night of the soul but also through the dark night of injustice.

Mariology was a highly contentious issue at Vatican Two for many reasons. In ascetic clerical cultures, Mary has become an image of the ideal feminine in the psychology of many bishops, including Pope John Paul II who lost his own mother as a young boy. After the French Revolution and the anticlericalism that new democratic political cultures brought to Europe, the authority of the church was diminished in public life but in the church in the nineteenth century, Marian devotions flourished. The first Marian dogmas, the Immaculate Conception in 1854 and a century later, the Assumption in 1950 reflected an active and widespread Marian devotion that had accumulated in the church as pious practice for centuries, claims that are nonetheless questionable in their historical infallibility as well as their theological intent. Most controversial of all in ecumenical discussions is the attribution, Mediatrix of all graces, that I learned as a member of the Legion of Mary in my first parish. In the Dominican Republic, Mary is called Our Lady of Altagracia. European Catholic ecumenical theologians at Vatican Two challenged this attribution to Mary, declaring that the Spirit of God alone is the source of the grace we are given through personal revelation.

For the first three centuries of the church, popular devotion was marked by the veneration of the Christian martyrs, usually through feast day celebrations where these men and women were heralded as models of heroic faith. Mary was not a martyr, and so there was no public, official veneration of Mary. In the fourth century, during the christological debates before, during and after the council of Nicaea, she assumed a new centrality in her role as the mother of Jesus. The docetists claimed that Jesus had not truly been a human person but that he had merely appeared in the guise of a human body, so as not to taint his divinity with the defilement of a material body, the influence of Greek, Gnostic and Manichaean dualism. Mary's maternity was called into service to defend the principle of incarnation, that the divine presence of God had entered into the human flesh of Jesus and that Jesus was subject to the same human finitude that we are.

Two predominant schools of thought issued from these very heated and prolonged Christological debates. The Antioch school proposed a moral union of two natures, where, as a human being, Jesus would respond to some events in a human way, thirst, hunger, weariness etc. and sometimes in a divine way, e.g. performing miracles. The Alexandrian school argued for a stronger ontological form of union in which Jesus' humanity was essentially swallowed up in his transcendent divinity, leaving a more docetist impression in the popular Christian mind until very recently. Now proclaimed as the Mother of God, the Marian cult began to develop, especially in eastern Christianity. In the fifth century, Augustine downplayed the exceptionality of Mary, despite his equation of sexuality with human sinfulness and his elevation of virginity as a superior Christian lifestyle, and presented her as a member of the community of believers, insisting that it was her faith and not her maternity that was significant. He situates Mary in the midst of the believing community, not above it.

Popular religious piety however usually reflects the pastoral needs of the community to strengthen their faith and to endure with hope the travails and suffering of our lives, not the clarity or logic of the theological tradition. As the institutional church during the Middle Ages became more preoccupied with sin and created elaborate legalistic penitential systems to address human sinfulness, the remoteness of Jesus now conceived as the divine Judge led to more elaborated devotions to Mary, the merciful virgin who could influence her son to human benefit. Anthropomorphism aside, as the merciful face of God, Mary came to be seen as a mediator, a *mediatrix* of divine grace, challenging not only the role of Jesus as mediator of God's presence but also that of the Holy Spirit as the bestower of divine grace. When official theological instruction loses its pastoral efficacy, the faithful find their own way. Dating back to the claim of

Bernard of Clairvaux, *that God wills us to have everything through Mary,* subsequent popes would echo this conviction, *that the Son will hear the mother, the father hear the Son,* in response to the pleas and prayers of the penitent. Devotions to Mary flourished, her name adorning cathedrals and churches, eventually becoming aligned with an elaborate body of pious liturgical practices marked by sentimentality and superstition, with the powerful mother of God dispensing salvation to sinful humanity.

The recent preconciliar neo-scholastic tradition presented grace as a spiritual substance, a sanctifying grace that could be quantitatively acquired in a rather Pelagian way through participation in the sacraments and through moral righteousness, in devotions to Mary such as the rosary, through participation in the Legion of Mary or the Sodality of our Lady and these practices encouraged a prayer and piety that often left the Trinity on the back burner. Karl Rahner. S.J., one of the fathers of Vatican Two, proposed that grace is God's free, uncreated gift of liberating and loving self-communication to all of his creation, an interpersonal and relational illumination that takes place in the heart of one's worldly experience, a communication that is part of the essence of who God is. Rather than something that can be lost through sin and regained through repentance, this sanctifying, healing and liberating grace is unconditional, everlasting and no sin could ever extinguish it. An expression of the divine universal saving will, this grace is not restricted to Christians alone but is at the heart of all the great religions of the world. As Teillard de Chardin insisted, nothing is secular for those who know how to see. History is the locus of God's activity, and God's presence in our ordinary secular lives encourages our participation in God's liberating and humanizing intent for all of his creatures, not just for those retreating into a cloister.

It is one's nearness to God through the Spirit that advances rather than constricts human autonomy and responsibility, and there is no holiness to be had in a lifestyle removed from the struggles of history. God's grace is most realized by those who take up the challenges of their particular place in history, challenging the forces of darkness that haunt and betray our ecclesial and secular institutional cultures, and diminish the quality of life of so many innocents. Holiness and the struggle for righteousness is to be found not only in the family or the parish communities, but in the neighbourhood, the educational or commercial institution or the political arena. Communal and collective salvation defines the Christian life, not just a concern with personal salvation.

Protestantism, for whom Jesus is the sole mediator of God's grace, challenged these claims of an entrenched pious Christian practice, and the Council of Trent attempted to correct many excesses. Marian devotion nonetheless increased, and Mariology split off as a separate branch of Catholic theology. In popular practice, the faithful directed prayers of petition to Mary as they did to the saints, and raised their children to do the same. In the nineteenth century in the midst of anticlerical hostility following the French Revolution throughout Europe, many new religious orders adopted her name: sodalities of young men and women dedicated to Mary flourished in parishes and schools; the months of May and October were dedicated to her crowning and to the Rosary, and Marian congresses abounded.[6] In the aftermath of the European popular democratic revolutions of 1848, in 1854 Pius IX published the first Marian dogmatic statement on her immaculate conception, and in 1858, Bernadette Soubirous of Lourdes in southern France, reported personal apparitions. The next pope, Leo XIII, dedicated eleven of his forty-two encyclicals to her. At Fatima in Portugal in 1917, three children reported another apparition, and in 1921, the Legion of Mary, an apostolic association of Catholic laywomen, was founded in Dublin, Ireland. In 1950, Pius XII proclaimed the second Marian dogma, her assumption into heaven. In Portuguese cultures including former colonial possessions such as Brazil and Sri Lanka, and throughout the Spanish-speaking world, as in Mexico and Cuba, visions and apparitions of Mary have been claimed by various peasant men and women.

But the women's movement of the twentieth century would challenge the image of female femininity usually associated with Mary in unexpected but dramatic ways. Progressive Catholic European theologians recognized the difficulties that Marian dogma raised in their ecumenical discussions with Protestantism, as both groups sought common ground toward greater Christian unity. As I have pointed out, aligned with the biblical, liturgical and ecumenical movements of the early part of the twentieth century, Catholic theologians sought to return to the original sources, a process called *ressourcement*, to determine a more historical validity to the claims made about her as they did for every aspect of Christian dogma and tradition. Bishops and theologians from the developing nations recognized the important symbolism of Mary's identification with the poor in the awakening social movements of the Third World that had begun in the nineteen fifties and were intensifying in their political impact in their own societies during the sixties and seventies.

At Vatican Two, traditionalists and reformers engaged in an emotional fracas over Mary that left both sides embarrassed and exhausted.[6] The traditionalists from Poland, Italy, Spain, Portugal, and the Philippines, favoured an emphasis on her exceptionality, titles and special privileges, pure, undefiled, etc. and sought a separate schema on Mary while the progressives from France, Belgium, Holland, and Germany sought to downplay the more recent Marian excess through a more biblical and theologically grounded approach, and to situate her within the community of the Church as a chapter within *Lumen Gentium*, the Constitution on the Church. The least unanimous vote taken at the council, these debates revealed a deep fissure in the international episcopacy, as a mentality of authoritarian orthodoxy accompanied by a piety focused on the world to come, rammed up against a church eager to enter into history and to engage the social and political implications of the Gospel. The attribution *Mediatrix of all graces,* was modified to a context of pious practice, so as to distinguish her from the Spirit of God, and presented the doctrinal claim of Mary as a model of the church indicating her return to the whole community, although this image has never caught the public imagination. In the document, there is no inclusion of Mary in the church's special vocation to the poor or to its opening dialogue with the modern world. The language of her idealized perfection was maintained, emphasizing her as a model of receptivity to God's grace but not of agency or of power but continuing the harmful Mary-Eve dichotomy and the language of subordination. Curiously, in the province of Quebec, where, more than any other part of Canada, all forms of traditional Catholicism have been completely overridden since the nineteen sixties, public Catholic schools eliminated and churches emptied and sold for condos, the most popular name given to female infants is the combination, Marie-Ève.

The present historical engagement of women to realize their own human potential and human rights has been formally acknowledged in the church. Fifty years ago, in *Pacem in Terris*, John XXIII recognized that educated women were demanding equality and dignity in practice as well as in law, institutional recognition and meaningful participation in the political process as well as a shared partnership in the parenting of a family. A decade after Vatican Two, Paul VI published *Marianus Cultus*, in recognition that previous expressions of Marian devotion had disappeared and he asked the international Catholic community to create new liturgical forms more appropriate to a changing cultural tradition, laying down specific guidelines: that biblical sources be used, that ecumenical sensitivities be honoured and the centrality of Christ addressed, and that these renewed practices reflect the psychological and sociological struggle for gender equality then taking place. He describes Mary as a strong and intelligent woman who knew poverty and suffering, flight and exile, and who had consistently made difficult choices in her consent to the will of God. Rather than remain silent and submissive, she proclaimed God's partiality for the poor.

Androcentric Mariology

The image of countercultural community presented in the gospels, and especially in the Acts of the Apostles is that of a community of equals rooted in the principle of mutual service and marked especially by an economic inclusion of the poor and of the social outcast. The historical evidence suggests, notably in the epistles of Paul, that the leadership roles exercised by women were gradually eradicated as the early Christian communities sought to integrate and survive in their various societies, accommodating the dominant patriarchal norms and familial structures of the Graeco-classical mainstream and serving their own traditional interests. Even the clerical status of female deacon was in time eliminated. As modern Jungian theory has suggested, the androcentric theological tradition about her reflects both the idealized and disowned male anima combined with the fear and suspicion of the female nature portrayed in ancient myth and literature throughout the ages. Within the community, men and women adopting an ascetic lifestyle competed with those who proposed the patriarchal family as the norm of religious life. With the arrival of monasticism, female religious orders permitted a place for independent education and leadership for women and roles of various kinds of service to the community.

Throughout the history of the Church, male authorities have sought to keep religious women in cloisters and to control their public influence, a pattern that continues to the present in some countries. The silencing of the voice of women in ecclesial institutions left reality to be interpreted in the tradition from a truncated male point of view. The developmental history of Mariology was accompanied by distorted claims about the female intelligence and psyche by celibate ascetic theologians and by married men like Martin Luther for two millennia. And so we have an ideological body of spirituality that is not only detrimental to the flourishing of women but that reinforces in its antipathy and distrust the constriction of female roles and behaviours by the religious men in their lives. Emphasis on the obedience of Mary to God has been used to keep women in this subordinate place, dependent for esteem and power on the family alone, and away from the public square. Interpreted through the imagination of men, the sacrifice of one's own self-realization on behalf of one's husband and children was elevated to a kind of feminine moral superiority. Intellectual achievement, independence of mind and of identity, and certainly an independent income, challenged this social ideal of family devotion and of personal self-sacrifice. That Mary might have been alarmed by the life Jesus had chosen and brought his siblings to take him home, that she must have struggled in faith as a mother concerned for the threat she understood Jesus to be presenting to both the religious and political authorities and to her family's safety, although clear in the gospel of Mark, was simply ignored.

A more wholistic theology of Mary has challenged these patriarchal efforts to restrict woman's expectation of human fulfilment by the limitation of her social roles. Recognizing that Mary is too important a symbol to be abandoned to patriarchal opponents in the Church, Catholic feminist scholars have turned to biblical studies and feminist hermeneutics to discover a more accurate historical interpretation of the understanding of her that existed in the early Church. For example, instead of accepting the male patriarchal emphasis on sin as disobedience, feminists define sin for women as any behaviour that harms the dignity and wellbeing of anyone, that violates an ethic of care through neglect or indifference, or through careless, useless, unnecessary pain or suffering. Mary's willingness to accept the invitation of the Spirit to the life God intended for her is viewed not as submission to the divine will but as an eager cooperation and confidence in the divine will, a whole-hearted fidelity to God. Her effort with her family in tow to take Jesus home from Capernaum is understood as her appreciation of the dangerous road of prophetic critique he had taken upon himself, of the threat he posed not only to the Roman and Jewish authorities but also to her family.

A hermeneutic of suspicion to all the historical claims made about Mary by churchmen has led to many new, rich and revealing insights. Women have been reclaiming the goodness of their own sexuality, and spiritual purity for women is now equated with the same singleness of purpose to serve God as it has always been for men. For Carl Jung, being a virgin indicates a state of mind marked by fearlessness and independence of purpose, an inner autonomy, a woman who refuses to be defined by anyone else. An ascetic spirituality that values detachment from the world and the pleasures of the flesh, that issues, not from a Semitic sense of wholeness and of the value of the family, but rather from a Greek dualism of spirit and matter, promoted by celibate churchmen unable or unwilling to take on such a rewarding responsibility as a family, is now greeted with much suspicion.

Contrast the life of such a woman with that of one who defines herself by her capacity for reproduction and domesticity, where motherhood is the raison d'être of her existence. The most telling outcome of such an existence is often the perpetual adolescence of both husband and wife, of a woman who avoids personal responsibility for the social cultural and political evil that infects the lives of her children, and of a man who narcissistically seeks a mother/wife to attend endlessly to his basic needs. The moral challenges of an adult life for both are exchanged for the material comforts of a patriarchal household, the educated woman's life reduced to that of chef and entertainment coordinator for the family, and the psychological pattern (and often struggle) of dominance /submission continuing to mark the central relationship of her life.

In support of the family, the local Church has not challenged the evil of sexism, this restrictive ideal of human fulfilment that benefits others at the price of the woman's own moral and intellectual development. Once her life in the kitchen could have been justified under the rubric of protected innocence, her life untouched by the *sturm und drang* of a professional career in the world. But in a post-existential and psychologically savvy western culture, no one believes this any more. Women who live their lives in a kitchen and live entirely through the lives of their husbands and children not only suffer from higher levels of depression. They never really grow up. Is it any wonder that Catholic women look to secular sources and models in this present engagement to realize their own human rights, to meet a personal moral imperative to utilize their own intellectual, political and social skills, to achieve a cultural and institutional equality as well as equality before the law? This emergence from the psychological imprisonment of the sexist imagination has been painful and difficult for women because their oppressors are often the people who claim to love them. This challenge to the cultural conditioning of a bygone age is taking place within themselves and has been enabled only by the solidarity of relationship that partially emancipated women offer to one another.

In this new paradigm, Mary has become a symbol of liberation, not of constriction. No longer the passive recipient of aristocratic, mythical and theological privileges bestowed by the male celibate establishment of the Church, Mary has become an ally of the oppressed, the denigrated, the excluded and the poor, the woman who lived in a world of great disparity of wealth, power and privilege, who lived in unhygienic conditions injurious to the health and wellbeing of her family, a world of high infant mortality and limited life expectancy, a world where the life of a woman was easily endangered and diminished by domestic and political violence, of illiteracy and civic powerlessness. She symbolizes the Jewish understanding that Jesus himself symbolized and advanced, that God bestows his grace and blessing especially upon the poor and insignificant, the anonymous nobodies of this world. From the beginning, Christianity has stood as a religious consciousness and belief system that embraced the slave and the socially insignificant. The Magnificat, Mary's song of God's identification with the nobodies has been transformed from an expression of dutiful pious praise, into a rallying cry for the oppressed and Mary is now to be found in the midst of this bitter human struggle. Not an individualistic enterprise for personal liberation alone, Christian discipleship has become for women an historical engagement on behalf of all women at home and abroad in the two-thirds world.

Johnson points out that the aristocratic European representation of Mary in Renaissance art derives from the painters' eager desire to please their clients, presenting the mother of Jesus as someone who looks just like them. The historical truth of recent scholarship presents the privilege of Mary as the privilege of the poor, of God's mysterious preference for the weak and insignificant. The vulnerable, pregnant teenager who could have been stoned to death is protected through the gallantry of Joseph to accomplish the divine intention. Like the Jewish prophets before her, she sets out on her existential journey, walking by faith and not by sight. Her song of justice, the Magnificat, signals her participation in the messianic promise of God's justice and plenty for everyone, over against the privilege of the powerful and the rich. As Dietrich Bonhoeffer insisted in an Advent sermon in 1933 before he was killed by the Nazis,

> *This is not the tender, dreamy Mary that we sometimes see in paintings.*
>
> *This is the passionate, surrendered, proud, enthusiastic Mary who speaks here.*
>
> *It is a hard, strong, inexorable song about collapsing thrones and humbled lords of this world, about the power of God and the powerlessness of humankind.*
>
> *These are the tones of the woman prophets of the Old Testament that now come to life in Mary's mouth.*

In the 1980's the public recitation of the Magnificat was banned in Guatemala by the government. Throughout the Latin American Church, Mary's canticle has come to signify concrete historical transformation, a divine challenge to the self-indulgence and comfortable indifference of the rich just as it did in Palestine during her own life. Like poor women all over the world, she stands up to challenge the political and economic oppression of her life and of the lives of her children and friends. This defiant and dangerous memory of a God active in history on behalf of the powerless comes *through* a Jewish woman, but not only *for* her. Jewish people have always understood conversion as integrity, and salvation as radical social transformation. Mary's words announce God's saving action in history in the midst of what Gebara calls, " the ordinariness of sin, the monotonous parade of injustices, into the habitual insensitivity to pain, into corruption clad in gold, into lies masquerading as truth." In the midst of the anti-kingdom, the Spirit of God is alive through the actions of men and women constructing something new, in the insignificant places where God dispenses his gratuitous grace, the extraordinary mystery in the midst of the ordinary. Mary speaks of the divinity as God is experienced by women with a passion for what is human, the same passion for righteousness that the prophets expressed, a passion for the poor

1. Sr. Elizabeth A. Johnson, *Truly Our Sister, A Theology of Mary*, Continuum: N.Y., 2003

2. Fr. Tissa Belasuriya, O.M.I., *Mary and Human Liberation*, Harrisburg, P.A.: Trinity Press International, 1997

3. Rosa Maria Gil and Carmen Inoa Vazquez, *The Maria Paradox, How Latinas Can Merge Old World Traditions with New World Self-Esteem*, N.Y.:G.P. Putnam's Sons, 1996

4. Gebara and M. Bingemer, *Mary, Mother of God, Mother of the Poor*, Maryknoll, N.Y.: Orbis Books, 1987, 1989 (English edition).

5. E.A. Johnson, op.cit., p.p.114 to 123

6. E.A. Johnson, *op.cit.* ,Vatican Two : Clash of the Titans, p.p. 124-131

Further reading:

Elizabeth Schüssler Fiorenza, *Jesus: Miriam's Child, Sophia's Prophet, Critical Issues in Feminist Christology*, Continuum, N.Y., 1999

In Memory of Her, A Feminist Theological Reconstruction of Christian Origins, (Crossroad, N.Y., 1985

Elizabeth A Johnson, *Consider Jesus, Waves of Renewal in Christology,* (Crossroad:N.Y., 1990)

CHAPTER SEVEN

A Spirituality of Engagement

A new spirituality for the laity is needed. Spirituality is a branch of theology that examines the activity of the Spirit of God. For the individual believer, spirituality always begins with the surprise of an encounter with Jesus as God through the Spirit at a time of God's choosing. God chooses us. We do not choose God but we do choose to respond in faith to the life God is calling us to. Spirituality is the journey of our lives lived in the presence of the Spirit, in response to the Spirit and in obedience to the Spirit's call in the immediacy of events that we often cannot control. Twentieth century Catholic biblical scholars have extended the ethical horizons of this journey beyond institutional self-interest to a social ethic that extends to the ends of the earth. Innovative and original Jesuit thinkers like Teillard de Chardin have transcended long-standing false dichotomies of the sacred and the secular to remind us that everything is sacred for those who know how to see. The world is in need of our wonderfully idealistic and dedicated Catholic people and we must educate our young to feel at home as well as socially, culturally and politically responsible in this secular world, and to be both intellectually and spiritually empowered to address the destructive forces at work there, not to reflect the social alienation of those whose lives are limited to the Church itself.

In North America, the Catholic laity are now an affluent and educated people who integrate easily into all aspects of society- culturally, economically, politically. And yet for an overwhelming majority, the begetting of children, the welfare of their family and their occasional charitable giving are often the only expression of the contribution that they identify with social responsibility. In Canada, the national Christian Heritage Party focuses entirely on the wellbeing of the family, where protection of the fetus is central to its political identity. This party is favoured by many traditional Catholics and fundamentalist Protestant congregations precisely for this reason. This limited moral horizon is founded on their experience of the parish and the perspective of the preacher there. Broader horizons often reflect higher levels of education, but more importantly, an alternative experience of religious engagement than that of the parish.

Even atheists appreciate the quality of a good family life, and often, as was the case of the Canadian broadcaster Pierre Berton, have many children. Even in the animal kingdom, offspring are loved and cared for. This is God's design. Christian discipleship is surely about more than increasing the size of a family or of its social status through upward mobility. We are the presence of God in our world. God's values are ours. If we do not participate in the struggles against evil conditions that distort and devalue the lives of others besides ourselves, their access to the same quality of life that we enjoy, educational possibility, social integration, artistic expression and appreciation, decent affordable housing, what does that make of us? Is there not a connection between constructing the world and saving it? Is this not the activity of God? It is not the place of the laity to perpetuate the social alienation of monastic norms that characterize the priesthood and monastic communities, of those in leadership positions who live entirely within the confines of the Church community, and who, in their silence and inaction, criticize the secular world in all its brokenness from this alienated personal stance.

Although absent from the early church, monastic spirituality has been unofficially maintained since early medieval times as the official standard of holiness in Catholic life. Even the dedicated lives of secular diocesan priests are measured against it. To shore up papal power, Gregory VII introduced reforms whereby a tradition of a more than a thousand years of married priests and bishops was replaced by the obligation to join the celibate ranks normative until that time only for monks, a shift in spirituality morally justified by Rome as a higher state of life and of ecclesial commitment. More truthfully this discipline also served the purpose of centralized ecclesial control over their personal estates. Although there was intense resistance by both higher and lower clergy, even a few popes to this new direction, this discipline gradually became the established standard of holiness throughout the Catholic world.

In the wake of today's sexual scandals throughout the international Church, the theoretical justifications for celibacy ring quite hollow. Through the psychological eyes that we now use to measure every profession, many educated and faithful lay people now view celibacy as a personal avoidance of a normal developmental stage, i.e. the intimate challenges of marriage, and of the responsibility for the rearing and education of children. They wonder why issues that are deemed to be "not spiritual" but are destructive to the humanity and quality of life of many, are ignored. To justify their social and political inaction, some priests insist that social reform is the responsibility of the laity as if Jesus was speaking only to us. What do priests do all day now that the laity turn to specialists to heal their marriages and their families? The mystification and moral elevation of their lives that celibacy used to provide, has dissipated as the Catholic population, shamed by clerical sexual abuse and exploitation, has become more critical in its assessment of clerical life. The indifference of most clergy to life beyond the Church has become apparent to even the most loyal of Catholics, especially when they work on these social and political issues with Protestant clergy whose Christianity is shaped by a spirituality of the Social Gospel.

In the late nineteenth century, European lay Catholics in France, Germany, Belgium, Switzerland and Italy developed a new moral imperative of justice over charity toward the multitudes of working poor. Adult lay groups and youth movements began to address issues of human misery in their midst by supporting labour unions and developing both urban and rural cooperatives to make life a little more bearable for these hard working men and women, and to empower local democratic awareness and agency. Following the initiative of lay intellectuals in France, Switzerland,

Belgium, Germany, Austria and Italy, Leo XIII gave ecclesial support to these new voices through the encyclical Rerum Novarum in 1891, after thousands of workers travelled to Rome each September asking for his support. Although these lay leaders and the priests who supported them were frequently undermined by traditional clergy and Catholic business elites, including Pius X, the first pope to come from humble circumstances himself, these new sensitivities of lay Catholics toward the living and working conditions of the working classes of Europe half a century later, eventually influenced the discussions at Vatican Two. As a small minority of bishops from Europe but even more from the two-thirds World now understand, this new appreciation of moral commitment to social and political transformation has permeated the lives of lay Catholics in Europe and North America in varying degrees although life in the parish does not necessarily reflect this.

Contemporary biblical scholars seeking to recreate the historical reality of Jesus' world and activity now consider a worldview that alienates the faithful from the world as dysfunctional to living out the Gospel. Except for those who choose to live a celibate life in a monastic community or in the priesthood, that is, to live within the Church, monastic preference has lost legitimation in the Catholic community. And yet I argue that the impact of monastic spirituality, the confidence that social and political problems can be solved through prayer rather than engagement in social struggle and by challenging the *status quo* through local parish conscientization and organization, hovers over the spiritual culture of Catholic life like Sisyphus' boulder rolling downhill. The effort of each generation seem to be erased by the next.

Jesus was not a monk and he did not preach himself. He preached the Kingdom of God, a utopian worldview marked by justice, peace and love. His Jewish religious consciousness was not preoccupied with the afterlife. The idea that God's salvation/liberation exists for the afterlife was a reductionist distortion that developed in the first millennium as the now centralized Roman Church became identified with imperial power. After Constantine made Christianity the religion of the empire in the fourth century, the church moved away from the example of Jesus' life and the dangerous challenge that his mission represented to the status quo, to an exaltation of his divinity, specifically as the Christ preoccupied with the forgiveness of our sins. The atonement theories that focus on the forgiveness of sins derive from this structural institutional shift.

Throughout the Middle Ages, as monastic values came into pre-eminence, new christologies were developed reflecting this theological focus. The concern of Jesus to liberate those struggling from the colonial exploitation of Palestine for the benefit of Imperial Rome became spiritualized into a salvation understood primarily as reward in the afterlife. This distortion of a central Christian doctrine eventually became normative. A spirituality that endorses a resignation to the evils of this world in expectation of heavenly reward is unworthy of us and has nothing to do with God. It might be excused in a medieval world where ninety-nine per cent of the faithful were illiterate, and the divine right of kings denied any kind of meaningful citizen participation. But this is not the world we live in. A spirituality that is alienated from society, that discourages through fear of personal moral contamination and a misbegotten condemnation of secular concerns, and therefore the participation of every Christian in social and political issues that address a grossly unequal distribution of this world's goods, or that refuses to challenge all the dehumanizing forces that obstruct human development and personal flourishing, is unworthy of a Christian people.

This disincarnate spirituality is now viewed as an avoidance of the underside of life, and as an adumbration of Jesus' teaching. Is Christianity only about the support and maintenance of high culture, of beautiful architecture and ritual, music and art? Where are the parish priests preaching about the need for neighbourhood involvement in a myriad of issues that impact on the quality of life, from the safety of children to fair wages to decent housing for the homeless and poorly housed. What does the presence of the parish in that neighbourhood signify to those outside the parish in the neighbourhood, or is it no more than a religious association, entirely focused on its own social interaction, internal life and survival? We have become so accustomed to a Church that exists only for itself that we are not even scandalized by this. Why are the clergy, higher and lower, not bothered by this?

A clerical lifestyle with a guaranteed income and housing, without wives and children, and without an investment in the quality of life for the next generation, does not encourage an engaged commitment to social change on behalf of the next generation. A lack of leadership by the clergy in many parishes is due to this historical decision to make celibacy a condition for priesthood. And so Christian life continues, even in the poorest nations, to be equated with the middle-class values that many seminarians aspire to, and for the laity, a focus on the wellbeing of the family, its increasing social status, prosperity and respectability. Such goals, while understandable, have nothing to do with the Gospel of Jesus. They may be Catholic cultural norms but they are anti-evangelical.

The corrective to these Catholic cultural norms so pervasive in European and North American Catholic culture is coming from Latin America, and from other theologians in Asia and Africa representing the concerns of the developing world. The theologians speaking for their people in these distant cultures have taken us back to the historical Jesus and to the social and political conditions that his ministry addressed. Nor is this new in the Church. As I have repeatedly pointed out, Social Catholicism, usually identified by indifferent clergy as the responsibility of the laity, can be traced to its original stirrings in France and Germany and Belgium in the early nineteenth century. Aristocratic laymen and priests, horrified by the impact of the industrial revolution and economic liberalism or laissez-faire capitalism, sought to align their Christian values with support for the masses living in squalor, and exploited by their employers. While there were noteworthy exceptions among the higher clergy, such as Mgr. Affre, the Archbishop of Paris and Mgr. Giraud, the Archbishop of Cambrai in the industrial north of France, the majority of bishops had little or no appreciation of their moral duty to provide leadership regarding social conditions. They lived in a world of social, intellectual, and economic privilege and in their preaching, advocated the virtue of charity to rich and poor alike. Democratic responsibility to create just conditions of life came from the anticlerical free thinkers and the Protestants. Today on an international scale, the media allows no such ignorance, and the majority of priests come from humbler circumstances and cannot claim that they are not aware.

In his letter to the bishops of the world a month before Vatican Two began, Pope John XXIII asked them to reflect on how the Church might be transformed to become the church of everyone, and especially of the poor. After Vatican Two concluded, some theologians and some episcopal leaders in the developing world especially in the overwhelmingly Catholic continent of Latin America, took seriously the challenges of John XXIII. In 1968, the bishops of Central and South America met in the beautiful old Spanish city of Medellin, Colombia. There, they began to examine the Church's moral obligation to the emerging voices of the poor as these were being expressed by new grass roots movements for change that were erupting all over their continent. This new *irruption of the poor* by the once historically silent and fatalistically passive was met in Chile and Argentina by a series of military coups brutally suppressing this claim of the working poor to speak to their own social and economic self-interest. The conference at Medellin was supported by new theological academic voices from Catholic seminaries and congregations that provided a language and a biblical focus to an activist Christian spirituality, to an orthopraxis, in contrast with the Church's historical concern with orthodoxy as its central concern and obligation. The news of these controversial discussions quickly travelled north to Canada and to the United States, and the principles of a new *Liberation Theology* were incorporated into the theological cultures and concerns of these diverse countries.

In America, issues of race, the role of women, the perpetuation of an economy based on the selling of armaments for war and indifference to the needs of their own home grown poor were at the heart of the bishops' debates. In Canada, issues such as discrimination against women, neglect of aboriginal Canadians, world hunger, and economic theory were addressed. A national committee was set up to examine the attitudes and alienation of Catholic women, especially in relation to ordination. In French Canada, this shift in spirituality took place during the nineteen forties and fifties, following the catechetical patterns of France where priests and nuns organized the young on the basis of social class – university students, workers, and farmers. According to recent sociological studies, this new spirituality that embraced social responsibility and action on behalf of the common good, gave rise to the Quiet Revolution during the 1960's, a generation before the rest of the North American continent. It is not insignificant that Gustavo Gutierrez was invited to speak at the University of Montreal on *The Church and Poverty* in 1967, a year before his own bishops gathered at Medellin, the meeting usually identified with the adoption of *liberation theology* by the Latin American episcopacy. The lack of ecclesial comprehension of the lay conscience, the refusal of a prophetic priesthood, and subsequent feeble moral leadership in Quebec proved devastating to the future of the Catholic Church in that province, from which it has not recovered.

As one of the fathers of *liberation theology*, the Peruvian theologian Gustavo Gutierrez has pointed out, "ours is a liberating God, a God of Life, an empowering God, not a God of the Whip," a reference to the Spanish conquistadores whose arrival in Latin America over 500 years ago devastated the native cultures and enslaved their inhabitants by the millions. The Spirit of God is a Spirit of Life and of Creativity. Any religious leadership or behaviour that suppresses creative thought and action rather than encouraging the risk-taking such living involves, has nothing to do with God's creative Spirit. If the parish priest lacks the emotional security to foster lay initiative and leadership in the parish, including that of young people, he does not represent the Spirit of God. If he does not encourage them to address the issues, impacting the people of the neighbourhood, he does not represent the Spirit of God.

In the professional culture of Catholic schools and colleges that I know well, if educational leaders do not encourage the development of free and independent leadership among their teachers, their teachers will not encourage such leadership among their students. If only hierarchical values prevail, if only rank and control matters, if only the accomplishments of the most talented students are acknowledged and celebrated, if education is about slotting people into predetermined elites, what message does this send to the majority with differing gifts to offer to the world. Evaluation policies could be constructed on this more daring philosophy, that each school culture supports an intellectually well-founded and creative risk-taking on the part of everyone. This is how moral and critical intellectual excellence is achieved in every discipline, and subsequently transferred to other institutional settings. A liberated moral action is possible in a school where creative initiative and a spirit of challenge is encouraged. A fearful and elitist authoritarian control has never created anything new or life-giving for the person or for the world he or she exists to serve. It merely salves the ego and the psychological needs of the ones with power and official institutional authority.

We have many impressive models of Catholic leadership in Canada's political life. Jeanne Sauvé, the first female Governor General, had previously been a leader in Catholic youth movements in Quebec before becoming a journalist of recognized importance. The federal Liberal cabinet at that time was replete with social Catholics from Otto Lang in Saskatchewan to Eugene Whelan in Ontario to Allan J. MacEachern in Nova Scotia, along with many French Canadians. Pierre Elliott Trudeau surrounded himself, in his cabinet and among his advisors in the prime minister's office, with thoughtful, sophisticated French Canadian social Catholics like Jean Le Moine, Marc Lalonde, Jean Chrétien, the bilingual anglophone Warren Allmand, and Monique Bégin. Pierre Elliott Trudeau had been educated in the elitist, conservative, anti-Semitic, authoritarian, and reactionary Catholicism of nationalist Quebec in the thirties and forties, but in the course of his education at Harvard and at the London School of Economics, Trudeau, more than any other, exemplified in his life, a transition from a narrow Catholic worldview to an international imagination focused on justice and equality of opportunity. He interacted with his political co-workers in a very democratic if argumentative way, always respectful of their views and never intruding in the exercise of their various portfolios.

Allen M. Rock, the president of the University of Ottawa, the college he attended as a young student leader, was a fearless and innovative Minister of Justice and of Health. Later as the second millennium began, he served as Canadian Ambassador to the United Nations, where he joined the Foreign Affairs Minister Lloyd Axworthy, also from a Social Gospel United Church family in Manitoba, and brought Canada's commitment to an interventionist policy called *the responsibility to protect* to international legal acceptance at the United Nations. The distinguished jurist, Louise Arbour, engaged in prison reform for Canadian women in Kingston, Ontario before becoming chief prosecutor for the Criminal Tribunals of

Yugoslavia and Rwanda. Rewarded for her courage and the moral prestige she brought to Canada with an appointment to Canada's Supreme Court, she resigned that position to serve as UN High Commissioner for Human Rights. All of these impressive human beings were educated in Catholic schools, and in many cases, with their exposure to the ideals of social Catholicism, they transcended the anti-secular, individualistic spirituality of that experience. It is also important to say that some of these have left the Catholic Church behind, because they find there little communal intellectual support or community for the challenges of their lives.

Now over a century old, social Catholicism is a biblically informed commitment, not to charity but to justice through social and political transformation. In Catholic education, students have been exposed to a more biblically informed theology than that of the past, as the historical Jesus is pre-eminent in the curriculum, and a new awareness of social evil in all its forms is advanced through the curriculum including the addressing of social sin in religious studies departments. This commitment to God through engagement with social evil extends from the academic excellence of the most talented to the participation of those with different gifts. I will never forget the students in a general level class at Cardinal Newman Secondary in Toronto who threw their whole hearts into every activity we organized with a generosity that I found breathtaking. We now assume that it is the teacher's responsibility to create a culture of empowerment so that as morally informed men and women, these young people will be able to confidently participate in cultural and political life, and provide advocacy in the struggle to transform our societies into more humane and just places to be. It is a spirituality grounded in the *divine reversal* of the Magnificat, where God's preference for the poor takes precedence over those with wealth and power. This spirituality bears no relation to the domesticated model of the Gospel limited to the unchallenging events that often dominate the life of Catholic middle class parishes. Is it any wonder that parish life holds no attraction for them? Such communities are adequate only for the socially isolated, the psychologically needy, the perpetually adolescent regardless of their age, and the theologically ignorant.

Social Catholicism rejects as normative any spirituality limited to a concern with personal salvation/liberation. It rejects any sacralization of asceticism or of poverty for its own sake, a practice that serves only the quest for personal salvation but has nothing to do with the active and challenging life of Jesus. Jesus was poor and acted on behalf of the poor around him. He did not pretend to be poor to establish his religious or moral authority or authenticity. The guiding organizational Spirit of social Catholicism is not exclusive, judgmental or authoritarian but inclusive, empathic and communitarian, and while liturgy is integral to its life, it rejects a concept of Christian piety defined by prayer and ritual observance alone.

In 1969, a decade before he became Pope John Paul II, Karol Woytila published an academic contribution to phenomenological anthropology entitled *The Acting Person*. His doctoral thesis had been based on the mystical theology of John of the Cross, but this volume emphasizes the participative dimension of Christian discipleship and a personalist perspective on action. When the book was translated into English, the work was censured by the Holy Office. When Woytila became pope in 1978, he set about reforming a number of the papal congregations, and in 1981 he appointed Josef Ratzinger as prefect to reform the procedures of the Holy Office for Sacred Doctrine, now called the Congregation for the Doctrine of the Faith (CDF). The shared appreciation of these two men for theological pluralism, i.e. that no theological system such as neo-Thomism should diminish the others, led to a new era for Catholic theologians. Yet their commitment to change the social conditions in Latin America did not stop either of these church leaders from their official investigations of the theologians of liberation or their official censure of the priests engaged with the Nicaraguan revolution in 1979. These men were doing nothing more than the Pope had himself in Poland with his important support of the Polish trade union Solidarity. To counteract these new expressions of the Gospel, Rome appointed unsympathetic and uncritical conservative bishops throughout the developing world who subsequently rolled back many progressive reforms introduced by their socially committed predecessors, because this conservatism serves the welfare and survival of the Church, if not society at large. Surely the welfare of the world is the reason the Church itself exists.

At the same time in Europe, obsessed with Christian complicity in the latent as well as active anti-Semitism that led to the Holocaust, the Bavarian priest Johann-Baptist Metz developed a system of political theology that insisted on political engagement as crucial to a Christian understanding of the Kingdom of God based on Christian solidarity with all those who are suffering. Metz has been a prolific writer with an influence that extends beyond that of more controversial figures like Hans Kung, whose focus remains the reform of the Catholic Church. In 1979, Cardinal Ratzinger, then the Archbishop of Munich, invoked the concordat between Bavaria and the Vatican to prevent the appointment of Metz, a former friend and colleague, to the principal chair of theology at the University of Munich, against the unanimous recommendation of the university senate. In 1982, now a papal spokesman, Cardinal Ratzinger published an essay criticizing Metz for being too focused on the future and for not being sufficiently interested in the past. Karl Rahner openly criticized this papal direction, and in one of the last acts before he died, sent a letter to the bishops of Peru in support of Gustavo Gutierrez and his version of *liberation theology*. Although there are now many theologians writing in this vein, it is generally acknowledged that Gutierrez is pre-eminent in the movement. For this leadership, he has been banished from the diocese of Lima to the more receptive American Dominicans, and now nearly ninety, spends most of the year teaching in American Catholic universities

In Gutierrez' Peru, extreme forms of poverty characterize the lives of 13 million people of 22 million, people who endure high rates of infant mortality, and high morbidity from common diseases because they cannot afford to boil water or maintain other basic levels of human sanitation. While there are still many Catholic theologians and clergy who would belie by their behaviour and their writing that an active concern for the poor is central and constitutive of a Christian life, for the Catholic worldview of Gutierrez, there is no salvation outside of the poor. Until he was forced to leave Lima, he worked in a poor parish in one of the urban slums. Despite his many books, he has avoided the Catholic norm of academic upward mobility. These theologies are contemporary expressions of the social Catholicism of the nineteenth century that have risen again despite the repression of the French and Italian episcopacies and of the beleaguered Pius X, because of the initiatives of John XXIII and of every subsequent pope.

Although this was not a dominant concern at the Council, concern for the poor of the world made its way into the encyclical *Gaudium et Spes,* directed to the laity. In *Populorum progressio,* (1967), Paul VI described how the Church could contribute a global vision of respect for the human person, a vision that situates human development within the Christian vocation. In *Laborem exercens,* deriving from his support of the Polish Solidarity Movement in its effort to liberate Poland from Soviet Russia, John Paul II addressed the dignity inherent in work, the right of all workers to organize to influence safe and healthy working conditions, and a just and liveable wage. In Canada, when fog prevented his meeting with the Inuit of the North during his extended visit of 1984, he returned within the year to recognize their value in Canadian society. When he visited Cuba in the last years of his papacy, when his health was seriously failing, he met with Fidel Castro, and seemed to find some diplomatic common ground. Recently Pope Francis played a mediatory role in assisting the American President Barack Obama to change its relationship with Cuba, to end the sanctions that have prevailed for more than fifty years. Pope Benedict also became very supportive of the activist spirituality that brought the present Pope to power.

In the great tradition of Jewish Messianism expressed through the prophets, Jesus announced in his first public address in a synagogue that he had come to bring freedom to captives and to the oppressed. In this perspective, an integral salvation is not merely something religious or spiritual for the soul but is understood as a passing from less human conditions to more human conditions, following the Exodus experience. Mary's prayer, the Magnificat, is also an expression of the *divine inversion,* that the last shall be first in the sight of God. In Matthew 25 to 35, the evangelist is very specific about what Christian life entails. The deceased senator from Massachusetts, Ted Kennedy, cited these texts in explaining the motivation behind his legislative record. The human dignity and wellbeing of everyone matters. Christian life is about service, not power. In these papal documents as in the First and Second Testaments, poverty is considered a subhuman state, and is not elevated to a spiritual virtue.

The prophetic tradition of Israel that Jesus embodied is a tradition where God is presented as the defender of the poor and of the socially and politically powerless. Ritual observance, our expression of gratitude for God's gratuitous love and presence in our lives, is secondary to this emphasis. How did this challenging lifestyle become a preoccupation with ritual observance and personal salvation, concerned with life after death rather than life on earth? When the evangelist Luke describes in the Acts of the Apostles how the early Christians lived in common and shared all that they had, he was not idealizing a life of poverty but demonstrating that even the poor among them were looked after. Goods are shared to eliminate poverty because of love for the poor person, not out of love for the ideal of poverty. This is the biblical and contemporary meaning of the witness of poverty. It is a poverty not lived for its own sake but as an expression of a Christian life lived in solidarity with the poor. Material poverty, on the other hand, is an evil to be eradicated.

Spiritual poverty is never an avoidance of the cross. To opt for the poor and the powerless is to opt against the oppressor, especially when this represents the blind self-interest of social, intellectual and corporate elites, eager to fault the victim. Gustavo Gutierrez' spirituality of liberation originates with God's mystical call, and challenges *"Christians paralyzed by fear of the cross, isolated in upper rooms, afraid of the scum of society and cut off from the resurrection banquet of the uninvited to stand with those robbed of life and wellbeing."* (Boston College, July, 2008.) It is fear that causes the fearful to abandon their dreams in favour of an empty realism and in the process, deny God's promise to create a new heaven and a new earth. The Church's task is to declare this new epoch and to provide cultures of hope for those whom fortune has passed by.

Faith, understood as an existential stance, as a response to the Spirit rather than as intellectual assent to dogmatic truth, is the opposite of fear and apprehension. It is a commitment to God and to human beings in the light of revelation. Fear destroys self-confidence and trust in others. Fear impedes compassion and keeps the fearful at a safe distance from the suffering of the poor and unwell, destroying the possibility of communion. A spirituality of liberation establishes a relationship between a struggle for the poor and the utopian vision of the Kingdom of God, and reassures us that God's Spirit will ease our fear, support our hope, intensify our confidence, and nourish our creative imagination, so that we can engage in this liberating process and bring with us the marginalized and forsaken who have been left behind.

The absence of a sufficient commitment to the poor in traditional Catholic spirituality is perhaps the fundamental reason why we have no solid or actualized reflection on poverty in the Catholic theological tradition, apart from the example of saints such as Mother Teresa, suggesting such a lifestyle to be exceptional and reserved for certain nuns or brothers rather than normative. This has led to a justification of the spiritualization of poverty in Catholic religious orders. For the laity, almsgiving, just like the liturgy, has become the palliative for non-action. Catholics who have come to reject this soporific evasion, often find themselves misunderstood, patronized, and misjudged, not because this perspective is wrong, but rather because it challenges the bourgeois ideal of Catholic life. Catholics who have moved beyond the monastic paradigm are often forced to seek their allies in other Christian traditions because, as broad and complex as the Catholic church is, there is almost no local parish support for lay people holding this perspective. The martyred Salvadorean, Bishop Oscar Romero was isolated among his own bishops and priests, who referred to him as *a good man but mistaken.* And yet everyone knows he was not murdered while saying Mass one morning because somehow he had gotten it wrong. Between 1970 and 1990, over a hundred priests, brothers, sisters, and bishops were assassinated in Latin America. Hundreds more anonymous catechists, common people, members of Christian base communities were murdered for their activities to eradicate poverty and injustice. Most worked in poor, rural regions.

When Gutierrez was invited to speak at the University of Montreal in July, 1967, he addressed the topic, "The Church and the Problem of Poverty." The Quiet Revolution was in vigorous ascent in Quebec at this time. The Catholic Church, and not only its hierarchy, was under severe popular criticism for its previous alliance with the autocratic power of political figures such as Maurice Duplessis and his government, symbolized by its ignominious behaviour during the strike at Asbestos, and the subsequent removal of Archbishop Charbonneau of Montreal to Victoria, B.C. for supporting the striking workers with recognition of their struggle through the provision of food and clothing donated by the faithful. Gradually in the fifties and early sixties a critique of the culture of clericalism developed throughout the province, and resulted eventually in the termination of Catholic schools by democratic vote, and a decimation in popular Church attendance. Empty churches in Montreal are presently being used to house museums or are being transformed into condominiums. In the remaining active parishes, teams of lay people maintain parish life while one priest is responsible for celebrating Mass at two or three of these. On the other hand, today the province of Quebec has the most developed safety net in Canada, especially in its support for working families, and for the rights of women. Poverty is no longer idealized but is addressed through democratic will.

In Ontario, the shortage of Canadian priests has been addressed in another way. Unwilling to include the laity in parish leadership, for decades now bishops have been bringing into the province clergy from other parts of the world, so that Canadian parishes are transformed into various ethnic enclaves. To accommodate this, native Torontonians strain to understand sermons spoken in heavily accented English and reflecting an alien, often authoritarian cultural experience. How can these clergy, all new immigrants, provide leadership regarding the issues of Canadian life? Of course the bishops do not expect this of them. So once again an ecclesiocentric pattern is re-established. To be critical of this direction in multicultural Toronto is to be accused of ethnic intolerance, so faithful parishioners remain silent, unwilling to assert their right to expect meaningful leadership, rather than liturgical maintenance. Educated, loyal and committed Canadian Catholics are entitled to church leadership from educated Canadian priests eager to address the evils of the society around them Recently before the demise of the Catholic newspaper, *Catholic New Times*, the members of its Board were informed by a professional fundraiser that Catholics contribute less to charity than any other religiously identified group. Why is this so, when those attending Sunday Eucharist are always being asked to contribute to one thing or another within the institution, still locked into a narrow social charity model. This is the consequence of little ongoing development of their consciences about the various kinds of evil in the world beyond sexual issues.

The good news is that in spite of a lack of moral leadership from the clergy, many Catholics commit themselves to performing what we used to call *the works of mercy*. I remember a Sunday sermon at Metropolitan United Church in Toronto, the architecturally modest Methodist cathedral, when the Right Reverend Bruce McLeod, a former moderator of the United Church of Canada, acknowledged the conscientious behaviour of a Catholic businessman who visited men dying from AIDS one evening every week. Canada has enjoyed the leadership of a succession of Catholic prime ministers in the last fifty years. Catholic social workers abound, although many leave the Church as their social consciences develop and they encounter the indifference of the majority of other Catholics to their broader social concerns. The same is true for many Catholic lay people in the labour movement or for many who run for political office at all levels of government. As they encounter secular committed social activists, their membership in the church becomes more and more irrelevant, reserved for cultural norms that reflect their identity, for the sacraments of initiation for their children, or for the Eucharist at Christmas and Easter. What a tragedy! And the ecclesiastical leadership wonder why they receive no support for their issues from these people when they ask for it, as in the legislation on same sex marriage.

Historically the episcopacy and the lower clergy have always engaged in the political issues that they care about. Official policy that limits political activity to the laity dates back only to the concordats of the 1920's with Mussolini and later with Hitler in Italy and Germany. To excuse the absence of the personal engagement of priests in social movements that address poverty and other forms of injustice is simply disingenuous, although it is often repeated. Bishops have consistently done so when the interests of the Church were at stake. The gospels have always been read in the light of new historical events and cultural movements. *Liberation theology* began in Latin America when theologians such as Gustavo Gutierrez lost their priest friends, in his case, Camillo Torres, to the new liberationist consciousness and political movements that arose in the nineteen fifties and sixties throughout the developing world, but particularly in the societies of that overwhelmingly Catholic continent. They knew that these men were reading the texts from the perspective of the poor, the perspective of the historical Jesus, not from the perspective of the hierarchical institution of established Catholicism eager to serve the upper and middle classes. No longer isolated voices, these men and women argue for a theology of salvation that places the dispossessed poor of the world within a framework of God's loving liberating Spirit. To suggest that God cares only about their spiritual needs is barbaric. Sustained by this Spirit of holy righteousness, by Mary, by Jesus, and by the communion of saints, this spirituality offers an eschatological hope to these people, to organize their lives around a transcendence that is not merely self-serving, but embraces a struggle for justice to advance the economic and human rights of all their brothers and sisters, and to overcome the divisions of gender and of class that contribute to their oppression.

This kind of moral engagement arises from a magnanimity of the heart, from a deep empathy and compassion, a reluctance to judge individual acts while not surrendering high personal ideals, an impartial exercise of care in the midst of our secular lives, not from academic degrees. In the gospels, the leper symbolizes everyone who is shunted aside from mainstream society. Each one that we encounter is to be welcomed into the banquet of our lives. Through a genuine poverty of spirit, and the discerning power of prayer, we are called into the wisdom of God and asked to leave our own wisdom behind. Exclusivism, elitism, a deliberate separation of social and economic class, these are the values of humankind, not the values of God.

CHAPTER EIGHT

Spiritual and Material Poverty: How are they related?

Spiritual poverty, a total disposition of one's life to God, is an important theological value. How did it become reduced to an interior attitude of detachment toward the good things of this world. Whose benefit is served by this interpretation? A spiritual poverty that elevates an attitude but does nothing to eradicate the scourge of deprivation, marginalization, hunger, illiteracy, exclusion is repugnant. Material poverty is a central theme in both the Jewish Scriptures and the New Testament. Material poverty is located on the level of the subhuman. The poor designates those who live in privation and social marginalization. One might say the entire Bible is a protest against poverty and injustice. The Hebrew prophets insisted that God is absent from the Temple when there is no commitment to the rights of the poor. (Jeremiah 1:1-7) God is not in the Temple if those trying to find God do not put into practice the commandments of life and justice. The evangelist John places Jesus' expulsion of those selling animals for sacrifice in the Temple at the beginning of the Pascal events in his Gospel, and heaves his rage at those selling doves because the poor could only afford doves for their worship sacrifices. Money had become the price of worship, and God a tyrannical and demanding presider, not the Father who liberates the poor from slavery.

Jesus is bringing to light in that event a profound deviation in those who claim to represent God, those whose lives are dominated by the personal need for social standing, *places of honour at banquets, seats of honour in the synagogues, greetings in the marketplace, and the salutation, Rabbi.* (Matt. 23:6) Honour and power give these religious leaders a power that makes them unable to put up with Jesus and so they turn him over to the authorities. *Only the one who does the will of my Father in heaven..... I never knew you. Depart from me. On that day those rejected will be termed evildoers because they did not feed the hungry or give drink to the thirsty. Matt. 25:31-45.* If our actions are not inspired by the desire for life and for justice, God is not present in them. *Seek ye first the Kingdom of God and his justice....Matt. 6:33.* For decades the Galilean peasants were losing their land to the Roman imperialists, and the Sea of Gennesareth was becoming rapidly empty of fish. Does any sane person believe that Jesus as a Jewish religious reformer was indifferent to these realities and only cared about the spiritual needs of these desperate people? To place oneself in the perspective of the kingdom is to struggle for the liberation of the abused and downtrodden. A spiritual pep talk directed to those in attendance is not enough.

This challenge calls for personal conversion. Conversion on behalf of the poor and oppressed is a touchstone of all spirituality. To know God is to act for justice. Without community support for this kind of conversion, neither the emergence nor the continued existence of a new spirituality is possible. Even so, there is a growing demand for a more authentic and radical Christian response to the degrading poverty that we are confronted with almost daily in the news media. Poverty is inimical to human survival and human dignity, and therefore contrary to the will of God. Pious religious sentiment and prayer are not enough.

The present efforts of Canadians to confront the dehumanizing conditions of our First Nations peoples have exposed the limits of money in addressing aboriginal poverty as it has become culturally entrenched. Poverty in Canada is a state of mind that can only be addressed through the cultural attention and social inclusion that schools and churches can provide: identification of root causes, emotional support, institutional resources, personal recognition and encouragement, and social analysis and political advocacy when appropriate. Genuine friendship is a powerful force in changing the behaviour of the most alienated and undisciplined, so that they do not end up in the penal system. In Catholic schools, to put the most difficult students out on the street without finding some institutional solution is egregious professional irresponsibility. God does not love the poor more because they are good and deserving. This is how *we* think. Similarly if urban Catholic schools are hostile to the presence of autistic and emotionally damaged children, we have no right to uphold Catholic education *as schools with a difference.* If we discharge from our secondary schools the troublemakers and undirected, what are we doing in education?

Dietrich Bonheoffer was a Lutheran theologian who was imprisoned and later murdered by the Nazis during the Second World War. *He was the first contemporary theologian to speak of God as powerless, as the God who suffers with the victims when evil prevails.* He insisted that any expression of religious activity that leads us out of the world is unbiblical. The displacement of God from the world and from the public part of life is unbiblical. The God who saves depends on human response, and he saves not through domination but through his suffering with the victim. *It is not the religious act that that makes the Christian but participation in the sufferings of God in the secular life.* God in Christ is a God suffering, and to share in his weakness is to believe in him. This is what it means to believe in the Gospel, to be a Christian. *It is not sufficient to domesticate God in religious sentiment or to bottle him up in a bourgeois mentality by reducing a Christian life to a belief in human moral excellence.* Even atheists and humanists aspire to human excellence in all its forms. Bonhoeffer called this deterioration of God's word a *bourgeois gospel.* Bonhoeffer was the first modern theologian to speak of the importance of seeing the events of history from beneath, from the viewpoint of the suspect, the abused, the powerless, the despised, those on the underside of history.

Catholic teaching has always endorsed an education rich in the arts and the humanities, and even the sciences, and in the personal quest for human moral excellence. For those appreciative of the international Catholic theological community, there is no doubt that intellectual excellence is highly valued and economically supported by religious congregations and the laity who send their children to them. The struggle for women's equality in the church is presently being led by nuns all over the world holding doctorates in the various branches of theology, scholars who are using their cultural influence to change attitudes. Most male clergy study theology beyond ordination to advance themselves institutionally, to become seminary professors before becoming bishops, archbishops, etc., and use the Church's fear about political engagement even in a non-partisan way to justify their indifference to social and public issues, except it seems when it comes to same sex marriages, legalized nationwide in Canada in July, 2005. Imagine the cultural impact throughout the world if this distinguished community of Catholic scholars believed that it was *their* responsibility to transform the world and alleviate poverty, *along* with the laity. One can only imagine what an impact such an engaged spirituality might have both here and abroad. Of course this would mean that priests would actually have to do something about those people sitting in their pews who are struggling to pay their rent and to provide for their families. And to assist those single parent mothers who did not have abortions but carried their babies to term, and are trying to raise them as good Catholics with hope for educated and prosperous lives.

In the midst of a frenetic organization of the annual student retreats in our Catholic secondary schools, a teacher commented that the word should not be retreat but attack. This sensitivity arises from an ecclesiology that is not limited to personal spiritual wellbeing. While no one denies the value of withdrawing from the usual pressures of school or of life to reflect on God's will for the direction and future of one's life in the light of the Gospel, a retreat should also be a time to plan together the collective challenges for the school, or in the case of adults, for society. Identification of the issues and challenges should be done together as a group, and strategies also collectively discussed and decided. A retreat should not be merely a spiritual tactic for personal growth and renewal, but a means toward a more generous, attentive, and socially responsive life. Prayer and liturgy should support this agenda of moral development and growth, not supplant it.

Theologians from Latin America prefer to speak of the God of Life. They propose the term liberation rather than salvation as God's design for our freedom, and insist that no one is liberated in this world until all are liberated. They also insist, drawing on the central Biblical themes of the First and Second Testaments from the Exodus to the Magnificat and to Matthew 25, that there is no salvation outside of the poor.

CHAPTER NINE

A Parish that Matters

None of this relatively recent theological consensus matters if it is not enculturated into parish life, and this must be insisted upon by the laity. The clergy have been aware of this paradigm shift for decades but in most parishes the nature of their leadership has not changed. Even with the arrival finally of a pope who insists that ritual is not the defining nature of sanctification, but rather prophetic disruptive action on behalf of the poor and marginalized, nothing will change unless the laity insist upon it.

Recently I was asked to participate in a downtown parish fundraising effort in Toronto. Prior to a national election, the political debate was focused on whether Syrian refugees were welcome in Canada. This issue was a hot one to say the least, as the Conservative Party under Stephen Harper was admitting only Syrian Christians and dragging its feet even about these. In October, a month later, Harper was removed from office largely because of the youth and the aboriginal vote, many of whom had never voted before. The day I spoke with this priest, I happened to have just finished reading a recent biography of the pope that had been well reviewed in the New York Review of Books, entitled *The Great Reformer, Francis and the Making of a Radical Pope,* and discovered that his analysis of the Church and his determination to change it were similar to my own. I have always been willing to assist the Church and I called to find out if the parish was organizing to sponsor a Syrian family. It was not. I was told by the pastor that the money would be spent on adolescent catechesis at the Cathedral among other things – my field. He assumed that I would not know that there was no adolescent catechesis at the Cathedral. A few days later, I happened to be driving up Church Street in Toronto and discovered that the Cathedral, a few blocks away from this parish, was yet again being renovated. This is the way that priests from neighbouring parishes build bonds with one another. He also told me that the parish would be raising money for the Syrian refugees, but not adopting a family.

No Catholic pastor in the United States would dare to be so indifferent to such an issue. In America, even Catholics believe that democracy begins at the local level, and that everyone is responsible for the quality of the common good through local action and individual leadership. Theological sophistication is only useful if its leads to action on the part of everyone, not merely to symbolic gestures or ritual observance. Ritual should celebrate this kind of active participation in the issues of the day, not provide a substitute for it.

If the ongoing struggle for justice is constitutive of true gospel living and an essential dimension of the preaching of the gospel, we must hold one another accountable for its implementation in our lives and in our parishes. As has been noted, the key to this Christological shift has been the work of Catholic scripture scholars all over the world where the meanings of the text reflect a new consensus, a concern with the salvation of everyone in creation, not just of Catholics. Many Catholics would like to believe that we are not engaged in a struggle with demonic powers, with powers and principalities, but that evil is merely a form of psychological pathology alone. Throughout the Gospel of Mark, Jesus is confronted by the evil forces of his own society, who sometimes are the only ones who recognize the unqualified purity of his goodness or the depth of his social intention. God's will is inseparable from his plan for the world. The way of the Lord is accomplished by people doing what is just and right. In the first three chapters of his Gospel, John equates the doing of just deeds with walking in the light, instead of walking in the darkness of the world's sin.

He equates doing justice with knowing that we are identified with God. The wonder of God's presence in our lives is that the divine goodness cannot be manipulated by us because we cannot control the relationship. To interpret Jesus as coming into the world to die, rather than coming to do the will of God, would be to place him among the world's most pathetic masochists. Jesus identified himself in his prayer and in his ministry with his submission to God's will, to God's plan for history, not only to the forgiveness of sins.

The idea of God as liberator of a people derives from the Exodus account in the Hebrew Scriptures, a variation on God's deliverance of Abraham and his clan from the land of Ur. These divine actions did not only address the spiritual needs of these people. Similarly God's presence is revealed in a series of concrete actions throughout the course of our lives, and we are called to embody, to incarnate this same freeing love in our relationships, and in our social and political life. The fullness of life to which we are called is God's intention for everyone in his creation, Christian and non-Christian alike.

> *I have witnessed the affliction of my people...I have heard their cry of complaint...so I know well that they are suffering...therefore I have come to rescue them. Exodus 3: 7-8.*

To refuse to act means that others will usurp our power to act. Selective disengagement and detachment from the real challenges of our own brief historical opportunity, especially when justified by false religious claims, inhibits the moral growth of the Christian and of the citizen, and damages public perception of the Church as a force for moral social good.

The rejection of democratic structures in the Catholic Church has implications far beyond its institutional health and psychological wellbeing. Religious orders have in the past half-century attempted to redistribute power within their congregations as psychological insight has revealed the limits to human and moral development that the previous authoritarian cultures, legitimated by vows of obedience, had bred and perpetuated. Not only did these internal cultures foster a lack of critical consciousness, debate and intellectual curiosity among priests and nuns. Often running educational institutions that were shaping future generations of Catholic citizens, these communities promoted through modelling a personal and collective alienation toward mainstream society that was entirely dysfunctional to the young people they were encouraging to advance Christian ideas and values in that society. In addition, Catholic culture presented no significant challenge to the injustice of the societal status quo. Much of this happened on a semi-conscious level. If the Church truly believes its role is to be a *lumen gentium* to the world, and if it has truly committed itself to use its institutional power and cultural influence to serve the needs of those beyond itself, surely this internal culture of fearful defensiveness and social alienation is unhelpful.

Catholic public schools in the Canadian provinces where they do still remain, exist to prepare the next generation to participate in public life, to be emotionally, intellectually and morally mature enough to exercise leadership there, and to develop a religious consciousness informed by the life of Jesus and the teachings of the Church. Emphasis on their personal sinfulness alone is not what they need to hear. People are tripping over their sinfulness in their human relations every day. Preparation and access to equal economic opportunity for all students is also essential to the curriculum so that the members of both sexes may flourish, become financially independent and able eventually to support their families as well as contribute to the social and political life of the community. The pervasive misogyny of Catholic males, generations deep, must be openly named and addressed. Appreciation of the arts and personal artistic creativity also matter. Catholics tend to take their lives seriously, to seek significant meaning for their lives, and to enrich the lives of others in various ways. Since 1968 in Canada, a series of Catholic men have become prime ministers representing the Liberal and Conservative parties while others have served as politicians at the federal, provincial and civic levels. The Canadian judiciary has also been well served by able Catholic lawyers and barristers. Similarly, with the medical profession. The Catholic laity has done its part.

And yet at the parish level, lay people have no real authority, even as a parish council. Priests cannot be hired or fired for incompetence or lack of moral leadership. The priests hold the final financial authority. In every other social and political institution, the laity have been found trustworthy to hold the highest offices, *but not in the parish*. Even attempts for an ordinary parishioner to reach the members of the executive of the parish council were blocked in a downtown parish that I used to attend. The fearful man who answered the phone had been clearly instructed. And so, psychologically adult Catholics avoid such involvements and the parish is poorer for their absence from the leadership team, or from the parish itself. Most do not announce their departure. And parish councils continue to draw the uneducated and the uncritical, essentially those eager to please the bearers of ecclesial authority.

For the majority of Catholics, the local parish represents their experience of the church. Those of us who have studied theology and spent our lives teaching the gospel in Catholic schools have a broader, deeper and usually more critical understanding of what the church should be at the local level.

This is partly because we do not want these students to feel as lonely in the parish community as we do. The culture and life of the parish is critical to everyone who regularly worships there. When a layperson is unable to contact the head of the parish council by someone whose official role it is to prevent such contact, something is wrong. It is not only insulting to the adult calling, but it is revealing of the autocratic leadership that rules with impunity. While church officials take some incomprehensible pride in the claim that the church is not a democracy- a claim I have heard many times over the years - the only justification in the tradition that they have for making such a claim is based on the Church's historical alignment with monarchy and empire. There is simply no theological justification. God is present to us indiscriminately, regardless of age, or social class, or educational degrees, even purity of heart. For some but certainly not everyone, the experience of the Spirit is completely unrelated to forgiveness for anything, but is a response to our desperate prayer at critical times in our lives. It is often our need and not our sinfulness that brings God to us.

After forty years of examining the great religions of the world, I have come to appreciate that God also is spiritually present to Hindus, Moslems, Buddhists and Jews. Being a baptized Christian isn't even an essential, although I am grateful for this myself. I believe that Christianity has a unique perspective on God, a more demanding one that is related to the prophetic sacrifice of Jesus, although it is a perspective on the nature of God that is sometimes as distorted within the Church as in these other non-Christian traditions. Ongoing biblical investigation is dramatically changing our relationship to Judaism as Jewish scholars are now frequently invited to teach in Catholic institutions and a more profound dialogue is occurring between both parties. The life of the average churchgoing Catholic is usually completely untouched by these developments, because the average parish priest is unaware of them or decides that his congregation need not address them, his interest in theology as an academic discipline having disappeared. Catholics are disturbingly accepting of the mediocrity of preaching that they endure or perhaps are completely unaware of the Protestant or Jewish norm when it comes to hiring a pastor or rabbi. Nor would most of them believe that they have a canonical right to good preaching and exemplary leadership, i.e. assured to them in canon law, because the invalid justification for dumbing down the laity is so omnipresent among the clergy.

The model of the Church as a perfect society, a model that was replaced at Vatican Two with the image of a pilgrim Church reaching out to a secular world, nonetheless continues to stymie development of a mature lay community at the parish level. The Catholic parish in Toronto continues to be a world where no word of criticism of the church must be uttered in a public setting. Loyalty is equated, in the public sphere at least, with an unquestioning loyalty and acceptance of whatever priorities the priests and their supporters on the parish council decide upon. Recently at a university parish that I no longer attend, a proposal to support a provincial cabinet initiative on poverty reduction was never brought to the parish council because the pastor had decided that he wanted their focus to be limited to the refurbishing of the church building. A few years before, under a previous pastor, the replacement of the roof had been the focus. Thankfully, the pastor after him showed no interest in fundraising. The church is presently used for televised daily masses, a secure source of income for the Church, apart from the collection plate. Priests fuss over their church buildings the way some lay people fuss over their lawns. It is all about the superficiality of appearances.

For those of us who have watched our friends and family walk away from the institutional Church after declaring a pretty accurate evaluation of the church's dysfunctional impact on their lives, this continuing *stuckness* of a culture that has no place for the emotional life of grown-ups but continues to draw into its arms the morally underdeveloped, the politically uncommitted, and the emotionally adolescent, feels like an open wound. Catholics who are no longer with us are often not the incalcitrant sinners the clergy would like to believe them to be. Rather they tend to be educated professionals, often social and political activists disgusted by parish indifference to the world beyond itself, and weary of the intellectual and moral emptiness of the community they find there, where religious consciousness is reduced to repetitious ritual, unchallenging homilies and charitable fundraising activities, and where women are used for organizational goals but not honoured as equals through admission to the priesthood or to other significant advisory roles The harsher, more uncompromising demands of the Gospel are absent in these parishes. There is no forum to even talk about this. To be critical of the *status quo* by expressing such personal alienation while still continuing to participate and support the Church financially, is to be deemed disloyal, unreasonable or unsupportive by the priest but also by many members of his loyal flock. The description of the Church as essentially dialogical by Paul VI in *Ecclesiam Suam* has been forgotten or ignored or never learned in the first place. Denial on the part of the clergy and refusal to talk about this is the norm, because this is the model that works for those in charge. Devout and loyal Catholics have learned to attend Sunday Eucharist, offer their stipends and expect nothing more. And the clergy privately commiserate over the lack of lay participation by liberal, educated people and mourn the loss of vocations to their religious communities as if they have never been told why this is the case.

There has never been a public meeting to determine what the people of the parish have identified as a priority for them. This is the meaning of the term dysfunctional when applied to family systems or institutions. A church becomes dysfunctional when it is unable to confront a problem that its members know is there. Instead, only those with power determine both the issues that matter and the rules that govern what goes on. The situation has become so severe that even if a meeting is held, only the passive and willingly submissive would attend. There *are* no rising expectations. Many priests and conscientious, often activist laity are aware of what is happening but are too paralyzed or unwilling to address internal reform. From a false sense of loyalty, everyone feels obligated to maintain group loyalty, although this does not change their pattern of privately resisting these ongoing campaigns for money. As is the norm in the dysfunctional family, the children must remain unquestioning, trusting in the adults and hoping that the concerns of those in control are not merely self-serving.

In the nineteen fifties, the French Dominican, Yves Congar sought the inclusion of the laity to address this clerical blindness, and identified this kind of authoritarian oppression as the reason why the Church is no longer in France the *locus classicus* of the knowledge of God. Widespread interest in spirituality independent of ecclesial structures has joined secular humanism as a more acceptable alternative. Restaurants in Paris hold Sunday morning philosophical discussions to fill the void in a country that has become almost entirely dechristianized by a Catholicism that had become institutionally self-absorbed through its monastic alienation and indifferent to society's needs.

Any social culture is complex. The social sciences have taught us a great deal about the individual and collective unconscious and about how these phenomena shape the internal consciousness and culture of an organization. The clergy are often unaware of these new insights, but there is a moral imperative on the part of the laity to act as a loyal opposition to the executive in correcting dysfunctional elements. Often the more active and concerned layperson is eager for acceptance and inclusion by the clergy and becomes part of the problem. More disconcerting to those of us who have studied theology is the unwillingness on the part of the clergy to digest the insights of the biblically informed contextual theology that has reshaped the way we think of Christianity in recent decades. *Biblically grounded and historically informed*, a once excessively divinized Jesus has become more human, presenting a more challenging and demanding kind of discipleship. On an international level from Jerusalem to Europe to North America to Africa and to Asia, the historical and social context of first century Palestine has been recreated through anthropological and critical historical studies by first rate scholars, and these new understandings are changing Christology and the spirituality that emanates from our sense of who Jesus was and what he was doing by appealing to God's reign in history. Even the American documentary program, *Frontline*, has taken up this subject.

Why is it that an institution that proclaims an incarnate God continues to promote a disincarnate spiritualism, emphasizing the religious side of a people without accepting a collective moral responsibility for the material conditions of their lives. John Paul II spent his Wednesday afternoon audiences for the first three and a half years of his papacy promoting a theology of the body, and he reflected this concern in his encyclicals and in his international pastoral activity. How is it that he came to appreciate that Jesus' life and values, surely the central challenge of our religious lives, included a concern for the material wellbeing of his people, their health, their employment, their social inclusion, and their daily bread when so many priests and bishops do not.

This reductionism of Christianity to nothing more than a Christian life equated, not only with the primacy of the spiritual but to a reduction to the spiritual, to an unhealthy pietism and angelism, results in a culture dedicated only to a bourgeois respectability that is hardly theologically justifiable. As the Christ, Jesus is our liberating God. Empowerment and initiative rather than control should mark the style and content of the community of the people of God. Holiness marked by the struggle for biblical justice rather than almsgiving should be the raison d'être of the parish community. Liturgy, prayer, retreats, biblical study groups, youth organizations, even the Rite of Christian Initiation for Adults must serve and celebrate this adult vocation to serve the larger community, to address the secular world, to become concerned with its multifaceted salvation as well as our own. The days of the Catholic ghetto, insular, "spiritual", self-absorbed are over. Like any institution, the parish has a synergy that is larger than any of its individual parts, but an inspirational religious, moral leadership is essential for an expansion of the communal imagination and programme. Liturgical aesthetics is not enough. And the laity cannot do this without the tacit support at least of the priest. Economic survival, a living wage, appropriate housing, a psychologically healthy family life, educational opportunity and success, even the safety of the neighbourhood, all are the concerns of the parish. Not just how many people show up for organized social events or the RCIA, although these are important in the city where loneliness is so commonplace.

In his analysis of ecclesial dysfunctionality, Michael Crosby, a Franciscan/Capuchin priest fighting for the integrity of his own order, claims that an addiction to a clerical celibate male leadership model prevails in internal clerical cultures and organizations, a shared compulsive need for power and control that alienates those within from themselves and creates co-dependent infrastructures, cultures where anxiety and obsessive patterns of thinking dominate but are eased by a reactive need to dominate and to control.[1] When the group think is insular, obsessive and disordered, and denial and a dishonest refusal to confront what is going on persists as a norm, feelings will become frozen because the fear and anxiety, the hidden truth of the lived reality is not acknowledged. Where repression becomes the norm, passion as an expression of personal commitment and freedom, will be undermined or dismissed. Frustrated freedom breeds anger and rage, and behaviours become even more erratic and controlling. A critical spirit reflecting an independence of mind or feeling is experienced as disloyal and shame-provoking, and therefore must be repressed so that the community may continue. Where there is limited trust and trustworthiness, paranoia, not just toward the secular world where religious authority and concerns are greeted with uncomprehending silence and sometimes disdain, but also distrust towards the laity and their intentions, becomes normative, anticipated, presumed.

The early disciples of Francis of Assisi were called the "true followers of justice". Francis wanted his community to signify the peace of the participative community of the Trinity. His emphasis on the sharing of resources was central to his vision. In democratic societies, the state is responsible for ensuring the sharing of resources through enlightened social policies to bring about social inclusion, fairness, affordable healthcare etc. and the state responds to the values and political will of the citizenry. If these issues are prevented from being addressed from the pulpit by an understanding of priesthood that eschews the public realm, and by a parish culture reduced to socializing and fundraising, how will the parishioners be inspired and encouraged to participate in the political life of their society.

Throughout the course of the nineteenth century in Europe, priests and bishops stood for parliament and became advocates for the working and living conditions of the disenfranchised working masses. The great German prelate, Wilhelm Kettler, who influenced Leo XIII and who has been cited by Benedict XVI, was proclaimed as one of the founders of social Catholicism in his country. He not only preached from the cathedral in Mainz but influenced public debates through political office. The recent censure of priests desiring to run for political office has a very limited history, dating only to the 1920's and to the Concordat signed with Mussolini in Italy, for obvious reasons. While today's educated and capable laity is not seeking to be represented in this way, this formal policy has in my view discouraged the participation of priests in social movements for change, and reduced their priesthood to ritual performance or to spiritual counsellor. This decision to sit on the sidelines not only adumbrates the moral development and leadership that such participation ensures, but explains why golf is such a common recourse for social interaction. The usual explanation for their non-participation is that the struggle for justice at home and abroad is the realm of the laity. I wonder what Jesus would think of this?

In our secular lives in North America, personal security is buttressed by the conspicuous accumulation of goods and of wealth, a culture of consumerism. When the concerns of the parish become identified with the status of its architecture, its music and the aesthetics of its liturgical rites, whereas the more demanding concerns of the reign of God are overlooked, even ignored, the *lumen gentium*, the sacrament of the Church becomes marred by a message that is anti-evangelical. Charitable gestures such as food banks, feeding the homeless one day a week during the winter months, or the ministry of the St. Vincent de Paul Society toward the poor, carried out by lay people, have replaced a communal search to realize the social challenges of the gospel. A hundred years after social Catholicism was founded in France and Belgium, charity still trumps justice in the Catholic parish. And educated, committed Catholic lay people look to political parties and other secular bodies to actualize the Judeo-Christian ideal of justice in living and working conditions for everyone because these concerns are of no interest to their Christian community. Indeed they are dismissed by many priests as outside their purview, as the domain of the laity. The responsibility of moral leadership for the social teachings of the Church by the clergy is denied or more frequently, ignored.

Challenging homilies are rarely uttered in a world where priests seek the patronage, personal endorsement and financial support of their wealthy and more distinguished parishioners. The Catholic churches of Canada have become the legitimizers of the upwardly mobile Catholic immigrant population and provide the middle class respectability that dominate the values of most Catholic families. Those in their midst who seek to serve the poor of the parish and of the neighbourhood are tolerated but hardly applauded for their efforts. Even in the Liberal Party of Canada, there are usually a few honest social reformers.

The *reign of God*, the central teaching of Jesus is presented as an entirely spiritual affair, as a description of God's freely given grace in revelation to those who believe in his capacity for personal response, that is, his gift of personal salvation to us. The reign of God that Jesus emphasized as his mission is not a political program but it is informed by a utopian imagination for our wellbeing on this earth. I have argued that this spiritualization of the reign of God reflects a priesthood unwilling to take upon itself the pain and injustice of the world, a priesthood that has internationally deliberately chosen to define itself by ritual, academic achievement and positioning, maybe a little personal counselling. This choice belies the fact that there are not two Gospels, one for the clergy that is limited to spiritual matters and another for the laity that involves engagement with the mud of real living. The reason the Catholic laity have not been challenged to follow a biblical discipleship, but to settle for a comfortable bourgeois Christianity defined by upward mobility and economic status is because this is the social norm among a majority of priests and bishops.

Detachment from wealth, from power, from materialism, from social status and success, even from one's own desires, detachment from whatever would deter God's reign or power in our lives, allows us to commit, to dedicate ourselves to the reign of God. Jesus identifies *worry* as the major emotional obstacle. When our personal and communal desires become disordered, that is assume a pre-eminent place in our lives, fear and anxiety take over. In the Sermon on the Mount, Jesus is encouraging his fearful listeners to discover the freedom and courage of the reign of God. When our desires become truly grounded through faith in the reign of God, through faith in the Spirit's supporting presence at the affective level, a wholeness of heart is fostered and holiness accompanies it. We become more and more detached from false centres of value. *Consider the lilies of the field.* God understands our needs and desires the fulfilment of them. *Strive first for the Kingdom of God and his moral order of justice and all these things will be given to you.* Storing up treasures involves the promotion of justice in our neighbourhoods, cities, our nation, even internationally, through democratic participation and leadership. Lay participation is not just about participation in the Eucharistic readings and other liturgical events. Lay people can also escape from the demanding realities of creating justice into a world of comforting and predictable idealism, of ritual and religious association. We are all of us morally responsible as disciples of Jesus for the quality of life of people within the parish and outside of it. There is a price, Bonhoeffer reminded us, to pay for grace.

It is worth remembering that before the destruction of the Temple in 70 A.D., the Pharisees were also lay people outside the official priesthood, the religious liberals of their day. After the destruction of the Temple and the death of the resisters at Masada, when the remaining Jews fled to Jamnia, the Pharisees came into their own as interpreters of the law and leaders of the community. These are the *whitened sepulchres* of the house-synagogues that are condemned in Matthew's Gospel because they have become too preoccupied with determining who does and does not belong, fixating on the Law and abusing their authority for purposes of control. As Jesus endorsed a table fellowship of equality and inclusion, especially of the unclean and of the outsider, and identified the Sabbath as the servant of human needs, not the other way around, he challenged the authority of the priests. When he returns from Jerusalem, he curses the fig tree he had identified the day before because it did not bear fruit. (Lk.18:35-43) Matthew writes in 21:23. *"Therefore I tell you, the Kingdom of God will be taken away from you, and given to the people that produce the fruit of the Kingdom.*" Jesus was not crucified because he maintained silence in the face of clerical self-interest, nor did he save his criticism for the back rooms as an expression of political correctness. He challenged the clerical consciousness of that time, especially their hardness of heart and indifference to the suffering of ordinary people. Like the prophets before him, he exposed their hypocrisy in rejecting the heart of God's law.

Yves Congar was not naïve about how religious authority can be abused by laity and clergy alike. His proposal for a more inclusive role for the laity was based on the recognition that there are lay charisms as valid as priestly charisms. Both have access to the "living water" of God's grace. While he supported the charismatic renewal focused on the recognition of the role of the Holy Spirit in our lives, he was personally uncomfortable with its demonstrative forms of prayer. But he placed his confidence in the ever-hovering presence of the Spirit in the Church and in the lives of the faithful. He described discipleship as "the unconditional gift of the self to the living Christ, with a deep sense of the radical penury of our lives, and a childlike trust and readiness to do whatever he wishes in us and through us." St. Paul expressed the prayer of the disciple this way. "*We do not know how to pray as we ought but the Spirit himself intercedes for us with sighs too deep for words. And he who searches the hearts of the faithful knows what is in the mind of the Spirit, because the Spirit intercedes for the saints according to the will of God.*" (Rm.8:16)

Congar's theological successors, those who continue to argue for a committed and prophetic laity in the Church, have proposed a christology that reflects a deep commitment to the example of the historical Jesus through confidence in the Holy Spirit. Not a theology of atonement for sins, but a Spirit Christology that embraces the world in all of its beauty, ugliness and despair. Jesus did not spend his life in the confines of the Temple, but on the streets surrounded by his disciples, by fishermen who could no longer fish because the Romans had taken the fish and by peasant farmers who had lost the best arable land to their imperialist overlords through expropriation. He did not seek the personal affirmation and recognition of the powerful and influential, but devoted his life to raising up the nobodies. In his every gesture, his every miracle, his every parable, he sought to heal and include, to liberate and to warn. People and their welfare were at the heart of his mission, not buildings of worship nor elaborate ritual. His commitment to the truth required that he be critical of the dehumanizing aspects of the existing system, and did not derive from a psychological need for power, i.e. to carp and control.

It is necessary to ask what is the primary task of the Church once religious enculturation has occurred. When we speak of the evangelical task of the Church, what do we mean? The catechetical enculturation of young people has been central to my professional life in Catholic schools. We want a Christian people who live lives of hope and of confidence in God's loving presence in their lives through good times and bad, but surely this is not the end of it. God's empowering grace is intended not only for the person he calls into discipleship, but for the benefit of everyone this person encounters during the course of a life, especially the neglected and the unimportant. A humanistic education and preparation for work or further studies can be influenced by prophetic values. For a generation now, lay Catholic educators have extended the moral horizon of young people to embrace the challenge of creating a more just society. Young people are particularly open to this kind of idealism, but they are still preparing for how they will live the rest of their lives. Adults in the parish are another matter. Men and women are often eager and ready to contribute to the issues of the neighbourhood in meaningful ways if the leadership inspires such activity and enables opportunities to be made available to them.

Presently most parish preaching addresses the lowest common denominator of Christian living and commitment - rudimentary interpretations of the gospels texts supporting a humanistic call to become our best selves in the weekly negotiation of the minutiae of family and professional life. There is nothing the matter with this communal encouragement but let us not pretend that this is the religious consciousness of Jesus of Nazareth. Jesus announced his mission in the wake of the Hebrew prophets, men like Isaiah who were called by God to purify the religious practice of the people. He never criticizes the fact of ritual observance and it seems that the apostles followed him in the celebration of the Sabbath and the various Jewish festivals. But these events were the decoration of his religious practice, not the substance of it. The Sabbath exists for man, and if a man is hungry, then he should pluck the corn to fill his stomach. Similarly with the sick and the ostracized. Life comes first. He sought out those in need, those on the social margins, those who were physically hungry and he fed them, to reassure them that God was concerned for their circumstances. He never obsessed over the deficiencies and moral weaknesses of others. When he encountered people like the Samaritan woman who had gone off track, he forgave her sins to bring her back into the caring community, but this was not the limit of his focus. He was advancing nor merely a humanism of the individual heart but a transformation of the society.

The discipleship of Jesus occurs when we personally identify with him and his purposes in history. What were those purposes? Endless adoration of the Godhead? The forgiveness of sins? How did a divine concern for the welfare of everyone in creation become deformed into an obsession with human sin? God has always been calling us to become the instruments of our individual, communal and global liberation. To discover the freedom of the sons and daughters of God. While liberation from sin may be a part of this, it is hardly the whole story, certainly not the heart of the Gospel. That is the call to evangelize, humanize, and liberate all of God's creation from oppression and injustice, from an abusive ignorance and inhumanity, from a denigrating and dehumanizing material poverty, freeing everyone of the least of these to accomplish the tasks of their lives whatever they might discover these to be.

Prayer, meditation, and contemplation involve an inward regrouping of our resources so that we might participate in the liberating activities of God, assisted by the participative and relational community of the Trinity in the spirits of the community of believers. If the community of believers is only interested in contemplation for its own sake, or for its own religious group, and not for the suffering and struggling people beyond that group, the community of believers has abandoned the plan of God for its own narrow and self-serving sectarian purposes. Previous to Vatican Two, Catholic family life was defined by sexual purity and propagation in this life so that we might attain the next. Vatican Two addressed this distortion of the gospels, partly because of new historical biblical insights but primarily because of pressure coming from socially active Catholic lay groups throughout Europe that had been forming throughout the twentieth century.

Theologians who worked closely with these lay people understood their love and concern for the Church, especially for its authority in a larger social context. Every document from Vatican Two reflects this newly appreciated sensitivity to justice-making on the part of the community. Fifty years later the issues have changed. In response to predatory priests all over the world, the Catholic laity have organized to ensure that the institutional secrecy and self-interest that allowed this scandalous state of affairs to continue unchecked and to strip the community of its moral dignity in the secular media, have become a loyal opposition to the church's autocratic structure. Ironically, without the secular media, the laity would never have discovered the extensiveness of this behaviour, and the subsequent and appalling internal ecclesial insensitivity to the impact on the victims. The cold reality of a leadership more concerned with its own financial interests than the emotional and sexual destruction that these morally irresponsible priests had continued to inflict on innocent youthful lives with impunity from the law came to be even more scandalous than the acts of the perpetrators themselves, and to destroy the trust of so many faithful Catholics.

Lay Catholics are now demanding more significant and adult structural participation because they have lost faith in the clergy as a body, although not necessarily in individual priests. In the United States where democratic process is practiced, at the grass roots of their social organization, as Alexis de Tocqueville reported in the nineteenth century, these lay groups are forming coalitions to insist on such participation. The leadership is coming from members of the Catholic elite who hold teaching positions in the finest universities and run the most prestigious law firms and the most powerful business corporations. These are not Catholics who will walk away as so many have in my generation, or sit on their hands as so many continue to do.

Recent efforts by the American episcopacy during electoral cycles to return the debate to the sexual issues, to abortion, same sex marriage and stem cell research, and to make these the litmus test for Catholic politicians by publicly denying the Eucharist to Joe Biden in Denver during the Democratic Convention and publicly condemning any Catholic running for office who will not commit to the imposition of Catholic ethical standards on the general population, has been recognized by Catholic democrats as the self-serving ruse that it is. A clergy that continually insists that political issues are not its concern, has not hesitated to advance the issues that define its moral horizon. And new Catholic leaders and groups arise to defend their public lay representatives from clerical attack.

The sexual scandals have exposed the widespread prevalence of gay men and women in religious orders and the priesthood. While the Knights of Columbus spend literally millions of dollars in California to marshal public resistance to civil gay marriage, the numbers of gay people enjoying the protection of a religious Catholic community remain a matter for institutional silence. Editors of religious journals i.e. *America* who raise the issue in their publications are soon fired. Official American sociological studies have determined that the percentage may exceed fifty per cent. A small religious order in Toronto is entirely composed of gay men. But gay men and women who seek a normal committed marital relationship are treated by Catholic officialdom as unreasonably demanding, even immoral when they insist that their human rights to lifelong companionship and faithful relationship be recognized.

Optional celibacy is now being seriously discussed and advocated. Since the altruism required for social transformation does not appear to be present among the clergy after decades of lay prodding, perhaps when bishops and priests have a personal investment in the future through a concern for their own children and for their children's children, they will develop a Christian theological horizon that embraces a passion for the biblical justice that Jesus criticized the clergy of his own time for disregarding. Then perhaps their leadership will reflect these larger extra-ecclesial concerns and the laity will finally benefit from the preaching they deserve and the practice God expects.

Jesus was killed because he refused to retreat into a false consciousness about the social impact of a Temple leadership corrupted by its own self-interest and indifference to the demands of God's righteousness. Eleven of the twelve apostles died violent deaths for the same reason, for their fidelity to the righteousness of the biblical prophetic tradition, the righteousness of God. They were not militarists or political zealots, but ordinary people who were concerned to uphold and to represent in their lives the perspective of Jesus on the Jewish betrayal of the weightier measures of the Law. They did not retreat into a monastic culture of educational ambition and cultural refinement. They did not run from the cross. The cross is a symbol of orthodox Christian living, and is the price paid by those dedicated to realizing the kingdom of God's righteousness in our midst. Naming and challenging the destructive social and economic forces that prevent human flourishing is the difficult truth that Jesus engaged in. It was not an academic exercise or something that could be solved by organizing yet another charitable organization to be run and paid for by the laity. In Jesus' time, the cross was a symbol of insurrection. Today it is a measure of our communal authenticity. Only the morally uncomprehending consider it an ornamental decoration around the neck.

Our Sunday ritual should inform and celebrate our commitment as a community to social transformation. At its best, ritual reflects the activity of our lives, and does not act as a substitute for it. It is not a series of performances for spectators, full of words that intend no collective action. Such ritual is a travesty of our covenant with God in Jesus. Maintaining Christian values and ideals requires a community of resistance, not a community of acquiescence and mediocrity of witness. It is a struggle against the idolatry of wealth and endless acquisition, self-aggrandisement and social acceptance. The parish culture should be a place where Jesus' truth about the real values of God is upheld, not betrayed. Honouring the truth of Jesus' life, the truth about God, means a refusal to participate in the perpetuation of lies. Secrecy, cover-ups, special interests, power networks that serve particular interests at the expense of others, all are hostile to truthful expression. Half-truths and the obfuscation of the truth serve the forces of darkness. Lies feed mistrust and corrupt human relationships, but protect the self-interest of the liar. False consciousness and self-deception permit the status quo to continue. The famous Russian writer Alexander Solzhenitsyn called personal non-participation in lies the simplest and most accessible key to our self-neglected liberation. But he paid a price for his truth-telling. Nonetheless, truth provides a starting point and a methodology.

For the Christian as for the secular humanist, truth in spirituality, integrity understood as a truthful, integrated life where our actions closely reflect our espoused values and ideals, truth in the lived culture of our institutions, is the centre of civilized living, of a just and dignified human culture for everyone. Only a person who lives in the truth and is willing to pay the price of it can grow in holiness, in the life of God. The danger of ideological positions is that people who adhere to a particular ideology feel obligated to ignore the contradictions that arise. Genuine personal and social liberation arise only from a confrontation with truth. For the women of my generation, it has been the ongoing painful realization of the damage of patriarchal assumptions, often based on misogynistic anthropology with its distorted perceptions of the female gender that continues to endure. For those fighting racial discrimination, it has been a confrontation with the systemic aspects of racism. For gay and trans men and women, it has been the indifference of the heterosexual majority to the destructive aspects of their challenging lives. For the poor and the homeless, it has been realization that Christians find it easier to blame the victim than to fix the problem.

At the time of Jesus, for the ordinary Jew, illiterate and politically powerless, almsgiving was an act of justice. After the Exile, the words *sedaq* or righteousness and *sedek* or justice took on the meaning of almsgiving. In the Septuagint, the ancient Greek translation of the Old Testament, and a text used by the early Christians, these words were translated as *eleemosure*, as mercy or care and *dikaiosyne*, as justice. As western societies have developed democratic civil institutions to address inequality of opportunity and quality of life through public education, public healthcare delivery, public housing, public support for retraining of the unemployed, political awareness and public engagement have become the arena to address social injustice. Political ignorance suggests moral indifference. There is no excuse for the absence of an informed political imagination in our media-drenched cultural environment. Yet in Canada, only one per cent of the citizenry hold memberships in political parties all together. Surely an ethical leadership on these issues at the parish level is a more noble aspiration than social recognition of the upward mobility of a family.

Léon Cardinal Suenens, one of the strongest advocates for increased lay participation during and after Vatican Two, wrote in an article entitled *A New Pentecost* that "it is time that we change our vocabulary and stop calling our fear, prudence and our timidity, wisdom, when faced with the implementation of the gospel." Condemnation of the prophetic challenge is easier than personal conversion from the values of this world. Jesus exemplified a willingness to accept misunderstanding, suffering and persecution in his pursuit of the realization of the heart of God. He did not play it safe. He did not advocate a religious practice dominated by social upward mobility, the endless pursuit of an elusive social status with a little charity on the side. He was too much his Father's son for that.

John Courtney Murray, S.J. described Vatican Two as a council of renewal and reform. Renewal is about ideas, about a particular vision; reform is about institutional change. Reform does not take place in a library but in the political arena. Reform is always political and genuine reform always comes from the bottom, not from the top. The appalling embarrassment of the sexual abuse scandals to the laity and to good priests, and the subsequent efforts by church authorities to minimize or to disavow them, has dramatized the need for significant lay participation and involvement in the structural organization of the church at the diocesan and parish level. Criticism is not enough. Nor is distancing oneself from the pastor and from parish activities. The widespread phenomenon of embarrassed and alienated adult Catholics requires action. To refuse to act changes nothing.

1. Michael H. Crosby, ***The Dysfunctional Church, Addiction and Co-dependency in the Family of Catholicism,*** Notre Dame, IN: Ave Maria Press, 1991, p.p. 26-37.

ADDENDUM

Because I am writing primarily for lay Catholics, and not for academic theologians for whom these ideas are commonplace, I have ignored some of the exigencies of academic writing. Much of the biblical citation derives from classes I have taught for many years. When I cite the original sources, it is to encourage the reader to read further, not to legitimate my views.

ABOUT THE AUTHOR

Linda Arbour was one of the first laywomen educated in Religious Studies at St. Michael's University in Toronto shortly after the conclusion of the Second Vatican Council. She taught in the public Catholic secondary schools, specializing in the development of new curriculum, reflecting a critical interpretation of scripture, of sacramental and developmental psychology, an ecumenical stance toward other expressions of Christianity including the major world religions, with a particular interest in incorporating a commitment to social responsibility within the educational culture of a number of schools. Her insights into the importance of a theologically informed Catholic laity issue from a life of activist engagement within the Church, within the schools, and in the various political communities of Toronto.